THE ART OF
RENOVATION

QUARRY

THE ART OF
RENOVATION

HOW TO TURN YOUR HOUSE INTO YOUR CONTEMPORARY DREAM HOME, ROOM BY ROOM

GLOUCESTER MASSACHUSETTS

QUARRY BOOKS

BARRY SUGERMAN
AND
SHANNON HOWARD

PRINCIPAL PHOTOGRAPHY BY ROBERT STEIN

First published in the United States of America by
Quarry Books, a member of
Quayside Publishing Group
33 Commercial Street
Gloucester, Massachusetts 01930-5089
Telephone: (978) 282-9590
Fax: (978) 283-2742
www.rockpub.com

Library of Congress Cataloging-in-Publication Data
Sugerman, Barry
  The art of renovation : how to turn your house into your contemporary dream home,
room by room / Barry Sugerman and Shannon Howard.
    p. cm.
  ISBN 1-59253-240-3 (pbk.)
  1. Dwellings— Remodeling. 2. Interior decoration. I. Howard, Shannon. II. Title.
TH4816.S845 2006
747— dc22   2005034122
                                                         CIP

ISBN 1-59253-240-3

10 9 8 7 6 5 4 3 2 1

Design: John Hall Design Group   www.johnhalldesign.com

Printed in Singapore

Cover: Heavy curtains and obtrusive visual distractions kept the owners of this dated kitchen from enjoying the beautiful view just outside. Architect Barry Sugerman remedied the problem—and gave the room a fresh, modern look—by removing the range hood and air conditioning unit, drawing greater attention to the windows, and brightening the decor with a crisp palette of white and black. The new colors give added drama to the soaring ceiling, making the space feel more open and inviting.

This book is dedicated to the memory of my parents, Lourraine and George Sugerman, who supported me in all my endeavors, nurtured my artistic inclinations, and provided a secure upbringing so that I wasn't afraid to try something risky for fear of failure.

Barry Sugerman

Contents

INTRODUCTION   8
Getting Started   10
Crafting the Vision   12
A Renovation Checklist   14

PART ONE: SPACE-BY-SPACE RENOVATIONS   17
Chapter One: Kitchens   18
  The Elements of an Ideal Kitchen   18
  Solving Old Problems with New Ideas   20
  Exploring Space-Saving Options for Range Hoods   24
  Looking to Tile as a Low-Maintenance Solution   28
  Adding Grandeur with a Barrel-Vaulted Ceiling   31
  Inviting the Outdoors in with a Patio Dining Area   34
  Defining Space with a Curved Countertop   37
  Altering a Layout to Enjoy a Lovely View   40
  Case Study: A Whole House Redone   44

Chapter Two: Living Spaces   48
  Using Drywall to Make Creative Changes   50
  Transforming a Bland Hallway into a Vibrant Art Gallery   54
  Creating a Dramatic Entry with Open Stairs   56
  Toning Down a Themed Design   58
  Enlivening a Space with Appropriate Lighting   60
  Creating More Storage in a Beautiful Way   62
  Case Study: A Whole House Redone   64

Chapter Three: Dining Rooms and Gathering Spaces   66
  Discovering Special Structure beneath Dropped Ceilings   68
  Raising the Roof with Coffered Details   70
  Adding Warmth with Wood Cabinets   72
  Case Study: A Whole House Redone   74

Chapter Four: Sleeping Spaces   78
  Promoting Restfulness with a Raised Ceiling   80
  Remodeling a Child's Bedroom for Sweet Dreams   82
  Adding Interest by Incorporating Build-Outs   84
  Case Study: A Whole House Redone   86

Chapter Five: Bathrooms   90

Adding Style with Natural Wood and Stone   92

Reviving Elegance with Contemporary Materials   94

Building Unity through Common Design Elements   96

Borrowing Space to Enhance Functionality   98

Distinguishing a Bathroom with Suspended Lighting   100

Creating a "His and Hers" Look with Vintage Details   102

Exploiting Angles for Maximum Impact   106

Case Study: A Whole House Redone   110

Chapter Six: Outdoor Spaces   114

Enhancing a Garden with the Soothing Sounds of Water   117

Bringing Harmony to a Family Entertaining Area   118

Meeting Building Codes with Ingenious Alternatives   121

Cooling a Hot Home with a New Veranda   123

Embracing the Mood with Color and Fun   126

Welcoming Guests with a Grand New Entryway   128

Using Water to Create a More Pleasing Landscape   130

Expressing Individuality with an Outdoor Sculpture Garden   132

Choosing Details That Can Stand the Test of Time   134

Reimagining a Drab Front Entry   136

PART TWO: SECRETS OF A SUCCESSFUL RENOVATION   138

Traffic Flow   140

Proper Lighting   142

Good Design   144

PART THREE: CLOSE TO HOME—THE ARCHITECT'S MOST PERSONAL PROJECTS   146

A Family Room   148

The Architect's Bedroom   150

The Master Bathroom   151

The Architect's Living Room   152

The Sugerman's Pool   153

The Front Façade   154

The Floor Plan   155

Glossary   156

Architectural References   157

Photographer Credits   158

Acknowledgments   159

About the Authors   160

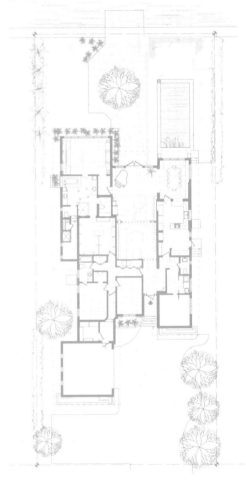

Introduction

This is an idea book, a collection of expert tips and hard-won advice from one of the country's top renovation specialists. Featuring dozens of dramatic home makeovers and clever transformations, it uses the work of veteran architect Barry Sugerman, A.I.A., to illustrate the ins and outs (and the ups and downs) of renovation and remodeling.

After forty years in the business, Barry is nothing short of a miracle worker. Though he has designed countless new homes, his true passion is renovating existing structures—specifically post-war ranch houses—by finding creative ways to make them more attractive and functional. A strong proponent of sustainable—or "green"—building techniques, he sees no sense in demolishing a viable home or erecting one from scratch when renovation can preserve existing materials and generate significant savings in labor, cost, and time.

If you share this philosophy, or if you're simply planning a renovation of your own, you'll find a wealth of information in this book. Created with homeowners, architecture students, contractors, interior designers, and other architects in mind, the text aims to explain and demystify the remodeling process, and hopefully inspire and empower readers along the way. Many of the projects are ambitious whole-house renovations—including lackluster 1960s tract homes morphed into sleek modern masterpieces—but each offers helpful lessons for makeovers big and small.

Whether you're dreaming of building an impressive new addition or merely tweaking the layout of your kitchen, one fact remains the same: successful remodeling requires skill, patience, and creativity. You'll find examples of all three in *The Art of Renovation*.

LEFT Form melds beautifully with function in this eye-catching foyer, where the removal of a load-bearing wall not only increased the room's width but also prompted the need for additional structural supports. One of those supports—a beam holding up the roof—is masked by the unique coffered ceiling.

Getting Started

Renovation is primarily about creative problem-solving. Because the architect is usually faced with existing components—electrical, plumbing, windows, etc—the challenge is to balance what stays, what goes, and what can be moved without breaking the bank. Rarely does a homeowner undertake a remodeling project without some kind of budget in mind, so the need to assess *wants* versus *limitations* is ever-present.

This can be a tricky process, especially considering the intimate nature of the subject matter (your home), so when selecting an architect, try to follow these steps:

DEVELOP A LIST OF LEADS

In addition to asking friends and neighbors for referrals, searching the Web, or looking through magazines, take note of homes or developments that appeal to you, and then find out who designed them. You can either ask the homeowners directly (most will gladly discuss their pride and joy) or contact the neighborhood association for more info. Another option is to call the local chapter of the American Institute of Architects (AIA), which can refer a number of architects who meet the requirements of your project.

Once you've narrowed your list, contact each firm and ask for literature outlining their experience. With brochures and bios in hand, you should be able to narrow even further, preferably down to two or three.

INTERVIEW THE SHORT LIST

Having the right chemistry with your architect is vital, so make sure you meet him or her face to face to explore the scope of your needs and goals. During the interview, you'll have the opportunity to speak about project details and learn more about the architect's background.

What is the firm's design philosophy? Have they ever tackled a project like this? What (and how) will they charge? Some architects charge a fixed rate. Others take a percentage of the construction costs. Still others set a per unit fee based on square feet, or even work at an hourly rate. It's essential to clarify this and other details up front.

ABOVE, BEFORE The timeworn façade of this home was crying out for a facelift. When the owners decided they needed more space for a bedroom and family room addition, it just made sense to rework the exterior as well.

You'll work so closely with your architect throughout the renovation process that it's essential to have a meeting of the minds. The architect needs to listen well, understand what's in your heart and soul, and then turn that into good architecture. In my experience, most homeowners really don't know what can be done with their home, so it's my job (and my delight) to show them that the possibilities are endless!

Within the parameters of lifestyle, aesthetics, location, and budget, even the plainest of houses can benefit from a thoughtful, well-planned makeover. I've renovated homes in a wide range of sizes and architectural styles during my career—from Mediterranean mansions to tropical Victorians—but I'm most intrigued by modest ranch houses from the 1950s to the 1970s, often overlooked because of their relatively nondescript features.

Our home was built in 1954, and by the time my wife and I moved in, it had already undergone three less-than-successful renovations. Each had made the house seem dark, boxy, and clearly dated, but thankfully none had destroyed its good bones. Any house with good bones can, and I believe should, be saved and improved. And by "good bones," I mean quality materials and workmanship. If you have that and a skilled architect, you can bring cutting-edge design to even the drabbest post-war ranch, and still keep your housing costs low.

ABOVE, AFTER While the inspiration for this updated façade came from a nearby house that the architect had created, the owner did put his personal stamp on this design by requesting crisp diagonals and sharp cantilevers. His "model home" featured more rounded and curving elements.

RIGHT, AFTER Remodeling opens the door to a full range of architectural possibilities, including uniquely shaped windows and dramatically defined walls.

SELECT THE WINNER

The best architect is the one who not only sees your vision but is patient and competent enough to guide you along the process. He should have technical expertise and excellent judgment as well as the resourcefulness and creativity to achieve your goals at a reasonable cost. And while you don't want an architect who will monopolize the project, only pursuing his personal vision, you do want someone who you can trust to be a leader and who can work side by side with you and other professionals.

Once you've made your final decision on an architect, be sure to outline the specifics of the project in writing, including the schedule, services provided, fees, subcontractors, and overall budget. This document should serve as a guidepost throughout the renovation, both for you and everyone else involved.

Crafting the Vision

The great Michelangelo was once asked how he carved the famous David sculpture from a block of marble, to which he gave a simple explanation. The David was there all along, he said. All the artist had to do was chip away at the pieces that didn't belong until the handsome form was finally revealed.

And so it is with designing a renovation. Many architects develop a basic plan in their mind, and then chip away to enhance the concept little by little. They look for ways to open up spaces, bring in more light, improve flow, and provide views, and then they incorporate design features that add character and work to break up the boxiness of an ordinary residence. The goal is to make a home seem more spacious and livable while also creating a sense of privacy in the bedrooms and bathrooms.

Every architect has his own process for crafting the vision, so don't expect a one-size-fits-all approach. You can look forward to seeing several standard elements, including a floor plan, various elevations, and at least one illustration (either hand drawn or computer generated). But it's your job as the homeowner to give input on proposed ideas so that the architect can devise a plan that's not only beautiful and functional but also personally suited to your needs and lifestyle.

OPPOSITE, AFTER Every home has negative space between walls that can be potentially more useful. By cutting into an extra-thick bearing wall, the architect was able to use this space to provide additional depth and storage in the new bar area.

ABOVE, BEFORE The curved settee in this corner reading nook provided the inspiration for a small bar, which the owners had been hoping to build for some time.

A Renovation Checklist

Before you toss your keys to a contractor or entrust your home to an architect, you should check on the following things to make sure everything is in order.

❏ **Money** Double check your finances. While this may seem obvious, many home-owners are so eager to begin remodeling that they start the project before their loan has been finalized. This is always a risky strategy. A better idea is to have the money in hand as well as place 10 to 25 percent aside in an emergency fund.

❏ **Insurance** Contractors generally provide insurance for anyone working on the site, but make sure that this is the case with your contractor. You should also verify the amount of coverage with the provider to ensure that it's adequate for injuries, thefts, or other claims.

❏ **Family** Before construction begins, talk with your family about lifestyle adjust-ments that will need to take place while the work is being done. These adjustments may include where they can eat and bathe and which rooms will be entirely off limits.

❏ **Pets and Children** Construction sites are dangerous, so it's important to keep small children and pets at a safe distance. You should also ask contractors to keep tools, supplies, and potentially dangerous materials secured at the end of the day.

❏ **Permits** Make sure all permits and zoning variations have been filed and paid for, and that the building permit is posted at the job site. A contractor who takes the time to file for a permit is not only abiding by the law but also pledging to provide quality workmanship and fair labor practices.

❏ **Materials** Confirm the start date with the contractor or architect, and then verify who will be responsible for signing for delivered materials. If you accept that responsibility, expect to verify that every item is correct and undamaged. It's also smart to have all materials delivered before work actually begins.

❏ **Trash** Don't assume that the contractor has taken care of trash removal. In most cases, because construction debris cannot be mixed with regular household trash, you'll need to order an on-site dumpster from your waste hauler.

❏ **Neighbors** Noise, traffic, and other inconveniences will likely affect you as well as your neighbors during remodeling, so it's polite to keep everyone abreast of the situ-ation. If workers will be accessing a neighbor's driveway or lawn, you may also want to get written permission.

ABOVE, AFTER With a work of art or a vase of fresh flowers at the end of a hallway, the mind becomes naturally curious and demands to explore further.

OPPOSITE, AFTER There's no question what the focal point is in this kitchen. The gener-ous center island not only dominates the room but also gains greater impact by mir-roring the shape of the ceiling recess above.

Do You Really Need an Architect?

A skilled general contractor can some-times shepherd a remodeling project from beginning to end, without the additional cost of hiring an architect. But there are situations in which an architect is essential, including:

- Gutting and renovating a large section of the house
- Building an addition or second floor
- Changing the overall style of the house (from Colonial to contemporary, for example)
- Altering the roofline or window configuration
- Making major structural changes

PART ONE:
Space-by-Space Renovations

CHAPTER ONE:
Kitchens

The Elements of an Ideal Kitchen

Up until the past few decades, kitchens were considered strictly utilitarian spaces—small, closed-off rooms where visitors rarely entered and only mom (or the staff, in affluent households) spent a considerable amount of time. Today, that view is much different. Modern kitchens, as you've probably read before, are now the "heart of the home," a place where families gather and where guests are always welcome. More than ever, they're increasingly multifunctional.

The ideal kitchen not only offers ample storage and workspace but it may also have a generous seating area, an open design that spills seamlessly into other rooms, and even a computer workstation. Other desirable features include a mix of natural and artificial light, pleasant views to the outdoors, good ventilation (perhaps with a decorative exhaust hood), and of course, easy accessibility. Every kitchen should be well organized, with utensils and cookware nearby and in logical positions, such as glasses near the refrigerator, knives near the cutting board, large pots near the stove—just like a professional kitchen.

In fact, the model for many of today's kitchens is exactly what the pros use. Many homeowners are replacing their small, outdated kitchens with large, open spaces fit for a chef. And they often want the appliances and work surfaces to match. If that's your preference, it can likely be accommodated. But even if you don't opt for that extreme, know that you can still renovate your old kitchen in a way that increases its usability and makes it a more enjoyable place to cook.

ABOVE LEFT, BEFORE Dated cabinets, limited workspace, and a visually obstructive column made this compact kitchen seem unappealing and small.

ABOVE RIGHT, AFTER By removing the column and making more efficient use of available square footage, the architect was able to increase storage, lighten and brighten the decor, and make the kitchen a more pleasant place to cook and gather.

THE GOLDEN TRIANGLE RULE

The perfect kitchen follows what's called the "golden triangle rule" of space planning, in which the sink, refrigerator, and range are positioned in a triangular layout. When designed correctly, this arrangement allows the cook to move around the kitchen in the most efficient manner possible, saving steps between tasks and avoiding any obstacles.

Solving Old Problems with New Ideas

Plumbing issues often pose as obstacles during remodeling, requiring innovative solutions to keep costs down. In this kitchen, where the sink was originally tucked in a corner near the utility room, contractors claimed that the sink couldn't be moved without interfering with the dishwasher's waste line. To solve this problem, the architect did the obvious—he raised the dishwasher, running the plumbing underneath. This not only allowed the sink to be relocated but it also gave the homeowner easier access to the dishwasher.

Another snag the architect overcame was poor placement of the kitchen's air conditioning ducts. Housed in soffits that ran around the perimeter of an already low ceiling, the ducts made the room feel small and also took up valuable storage space. A concrete slab foundation made it impossible to run them below, so the architect followed his philosophy that if you can't hide something, you might as well play it up. Fashioning a striking, v-shaped soffit down the center of the ceiling, he easily concealed the ductwork and used the opportunity to add stylish lighting as well. Continuous cove fixtures span the soffit, sending ambient light upward while recessed down lighting provides perfect illumination for work surfaces.

With the ductwork repositioned, more space was readily available for cabinets and appliances, thus increasing the kitchen's storage capacity and improving its general layout. Streamlined wood cabinets accented by stainless steel further enhance the sense of space and make the room feel more modern and functional.

LEFT CLOCKWISE FROM TOP, BEFORE
Dark, disorganized, and inefficient as a workspace, this dated kitchen demanded a total overhaul; Just beyond the kitchen is a beautiful ocean view but this layout failed to take advantage of it; Open shelving limited the kitchen's overall storage capacity, leading to clutter on the countertops.

Reflective surfaces bring a sense of vitality to a kitchen.

ABOVE, AFTER The renovation achieved a number of goals, including creating extra storage space, improving lighting, replacing the mica countertops with more durable granite, and incorporating a convenient desk area.

ABOVE, AFTER Moving the sink from its awkward corner position to an open peninsula allowed the homeowners to better enjoy the lovely ocean view.

OPPOSITE, AFTER Reflective surfaces such as polished granite, marble and stainless steel add life and vitality to the kitchen, not to mention durability.

Advice from the Architect...

I believe that today's kitchen is the living room of the home. Sometimes I even design it as a hub in the center of the house, and I often encourage clients to make sure that all their utilitarian items are also pleasing to the eye. When they buy a towel holder or a knife rack or an exhaust hood, I tell them to think of each item as a decorative accessory because the kitchen isn't just about food anymore. It's a gathering place for everyone in the family and any addition of attractive items will just make it brighter, happier, and more efficient.

Exploring Space-Saving Options for Range Hoods

Twenty-five years past its prime, this timeworn kitchen often served as a home base for its philanthropic owners' large charity dinner parties. Between fifty and 150 guests frequently filled its sizable footprint, despite a few less-than-ideal features and a largely dated decor. Although the functional layout of the space was quite good, the dark brown cabinets and prominent range hood absolutely had to go. Other problems included a plain vanilla ceiling and overly conspicuous air conditioning grills.

Challenged to preserve the existing flow of the room, the architect aimed to update and enliven the kitchen without really changing its overall design. Maintaining the original extra-long span of cabinets, he broke up the monotony by bowing out the countertops near the sinks and range and adding small columns in between appliances. Replacing the dark wood with bird's-eye maple, he also brought freshness and light to the space, making it feel instantly modern.

In the center of the kitchen, where the cumbersome down-draft hood had served as an unsavory focal point, a new, more attractive hood was installed, and the island below was enlarged to accommodate more seating. Ribbed glass cabinet fronts, strategically placed throughout the room, help to break up the expanse of wood while oversized stainless steel pulls complement the reflective quality of the new hood and reinforce the kitchen's contemporary style.

LEFT, BEFORE A wall of imposing cabinets, veneered in dark simulated wood laminate, made this otherwise roomy kitchen feel small and heavy. The squared-off countertops also posed a collision hazard for the homeowners, who were forever bumping their hips.

OPPOSITE, AFTER A 3" (8 cm) bullnose edge makes the counters in this busy walkway safer and ultimately more appealing. Task lighting, tucked quietly beneath the wooden soffit, provides drama and added radiance.

LEFT, BEFORE Rising obtrusively from the center of an island, the range hood placed an imposing barrier between guests and the chef. It also reflected the generally outdated design of this family kitchen.

OPPOSITE, AFTER Floating wood soffits and a modestly proportioned stepped ceiling helped to bring upward interest to the kitchen while French limestone floors and backsplashes added rich texture at eye level and below.

Obstacles jar the eye, disrupting the visual flow in a kitchen.

Looking to Tile as a
Low-Maintenance Solution

By the time an architect was called in to revamp this lifeless kitchen, almost nothing about it was desirable. Depressing, inefficient, and outdated, the room was colorless and cramped, with virtually no counter space. The ceiling was out of sorts, marked by an awkward level change, and the lighting (all fluorescent) was spotty at best. No doubt about it, this place needed help!

To address the ceiling issue without breaking the bank, a mounted display shelf was installed to conceal the defect. Along with new bird's-eye maple cabinets, the quick fix dramatically bolstered storage space and helped to soften and update the decor. In contrast to the wood surfaces, which bring warmth and character to the room, blue pearl granite countertops were added for a splash of whimsy. The bold blue palette, echoed in tile backsplashes and a patterned tile and granite floor, enlivens the space and yet still keeps it neutral enough to last for years. The tilework is also incredibly low-maintenance—a boon to an active family.

In the center of the kitchen, where an island previously stood, another island took its place, but with substantially more flair and function. Offering storage space below and a large work surface up top, the island serves as an ideal food prep area, with the sink and stove just steps away. The sink, which had faced a blank wall, now rests on a countertop peninsula overlooking fabulous outdoor view.

TOP LEFT, BEFORE Low ceilings, fluorescent lights, and dark brown cabinets did nothing to make this kitchen an enjoyable place to prepare food or spend time with family.

BOTTOM LEFT, BEFORE A typical 1970s kitchen with harvest yellow appliances and heavy brown-tiled floors, nothing about this space said "fresh and modern."

OPPOSITE, AFTER An obtrusive bearing wall on the southeast corner of the kitchen could not be moved, so it was incorporated into the new broom closet (back, right) and covered in cabinetry. An unnecessary "dummy" wall on the north side of the space was completely removed.

ABOVE, AFTER For a pleasing yet efficient level of diffused light throughout the space, surface-mounted ceiling fixtures were installed within a grid of maple trim. Additional task lighting comes from unobtrusive halogens tucked underneath the cabinets.

Adding Grandeur with a Barrel-Vaulted Ceiling

At first glance, this kitchen didn't seem all that bad. Yes, the cabinets and backsplash were a bit dated, but the overall layout was perfectly functional. The owners hoped for a larger space—one that enabled the kitchen to spill graciously into adjoining rooms—but they felt that the "bones" were still pretty good. Leaving most of the appliances in their original locations, larger structural elements, including the ceiling, window, and walls, received the most dramatic change.

TOP RIGHT, BEFORE A long wall of open shelving left ample room for displaying personal treasures, but it did little to open the kitchen to surrounding rooms, leaving the space feeling confined and small.

BOTTOM RIGHT, BEFORE Jet black cabinets adorned with large, garish handles overwhelmed the decor while a small window revealed a not-so-pleasant view. The looming old range hood also seemed quite ominous.

ABOVE, AFTER A combination of exotic woods was used to fashion the urbane look of the cabinets. Bullnose teak frames outline the sapele pommele doors and drawers, with dark-stained mahogany reveals in between.

OPPOSITE, AFTER Iridescent glass tiles grace the earth-toned backsplash while a stainless steel hood draws the eye upward and emphasizes the spaciousness of the new kitchen.

The ceiling, formerly low and flat, was lifted to new heights with the restructuring of pre-fab wood trusses, newly shaped to support a barrel-vaulted ceiling. Spanning the length of the kitchen, and uplit with ambiance-inducing lighting, the barrel adds an air of sophistication and surprise to the room, not to mention a sense of openness. A garden window, shaped to mirror the outline of the ceiling, provides a continuity of form as well as softly filtered natural light and a spectacular view of a garden fountain.

In another corner, double biparting sliding doors stand where a wall once rested, offering easy access to the nearby dining room and pool area. And at the heart of the kitchen, situated beneath a grand stainless steel range hood, a semi-circular, raised glass eating ledge provides ample dining space for six. Perched delicately above a granite countertop, it offers a new twist on a traditional breakfast bar.

Inviting the Outdoors in with a Patio Dining Area

Needing more space for dining and food preparation but not sure where to find it, the owners of this cramped 1970s kitchen sought the advice of an architect. Faced with dark wooden beams, a low ceiling, and fluorescent lighting that cast an unappetizing bluish shade on the room, they were eager to move into modern times. Luckily, an adjoining covered patio afforded the ideal space for their renovation. Rarely used by the family, it offered ample square footage to accommodate a breakfast nook, a small office area, and a generous buffet.

With French doors spanning one wall, the newly imagined room was designed to spill easily into the outdoor pool area, with clerestory windows on the remaining walls visually expanding the space and welcoming in natural light. In the kitchen, where the sink was repositioned to take advantage of the view, a multiuse peninsula and swinging-door pantry were constructed to deliver added functionality. Because the flow of the kitchen was redirected by these changes, the homeowners were rewarded with easier access to cooking supplies and appliances and substantially more elbow room.

Decor-wise, a striking range hood, crisp and contemporary in its styling, was employed as a cool counterbalance to the warmth of the cherry wood cabinets while elegant Juparana granite was installed as much for its beauty as its durability. Covering the backsplashes and counters, the richly veined stone radiates timeless elegance and acts almost like a work of art.

ABOVE LEFT, BEFORE A lack of functional space turned this cramped kitchen into a catch-all for clutter, rendering it virtually useless and visually unappealing.

ABOVE RIGHT, BEFORE Unmet potential was the theme of this bland breakfast area. Despite offering an inviting view of the pool area, its ability to serve as a focal point was never fully realized.

ABOVE, AFTER To balance the abundance of wood surfaces in the kitchen and breakfast room, sleek modern light fixtures and upholstered chairs were integrated into the decor, allowing the space to feel rich and warm, but not overpowering.

ABOVE, AFTER Outfitted with a salad sink and seating for two, this storage-rich peninsula serves as the hub of this busy family kitchen, providing ample space for meal preparation, food service, and casual dining.

Defining Space with a Curved Countertop

There was nothing special about this typical builder's kitchen: a dark, boxy space marked by grasscloth wallpaper, knotty-pine accents, and loads of white laminate. A long central island served as the family's primary dining area, and they enjoyed the convenience it provided. But because the island also dominated the room, resting way too close to the refrigerator and standing as a physical barrier between the oven and the stove, the homeowners decided that it needed to be reworked. At the same time, they also hoped to infuse the bland kitchen with personality, giving it a fresh, modern facelift that vibrantly conveyed contemporary style and functionality.

TOP RIGHT, BEFORE This dated kitchen had decent lighting near cooking areas but none above the dining portion of the island, leaving a whole corner of the room poorly illuminated. A brown-tone color palette made matters even worse.

BOTTOM RIGHT, BEFORE Even with a pretty poolside view, this kitchen couldn't escape the ravages of time. Stock countertops and aging appliances revealed quite readily that the space needed a good renovation.

To boost square footage, a bump-out addition was built to accommodate a small break-fast nook, which meant the island no longer needed to serve as a dining surface and could be reconfigured to handle just food prep and storage. Though it remained at the heart of the kitchen, the island was made over with a new stove and a streamlined appearance, and the stove was centered to allow more workspace on either side. Bonus seating came in the form of a new curved countertop, which was designed to bow gently around the sink area and form a sleek bar. Lined with comfortable stools and capped off with display shelving, it offers a convenient family gathering space close to the kitchen action, but far enough removed so as not to not impede the chef's progress.

ABOVE, AFTER A wood-framed bulletin board serves as a central family message station, leaving the refrigerator free of clutter. Recesses in the island discreetly conceal a wine cooler and other storage compartments, making optimal use of otherwise dead space.

OPPOSITE, AFTER Task lighting was greatly improved with the installation of hanging pendants and recessed high hats spanning the entire length of the room. The floor, formerly covered in 12" x 12" (30 x 30 cm) tile, took on a dramatic turn with 24" x 24" (61 x 61 cm) marble slabs.

Altering a Layout to Enjoy a Lovely View

Though this three-story townhouse sits directly adjacent to a stunning waterway, its original layout didn't allow for a clear view of that gorgeous vista. As you entered the front door, all you could see was the kitchen, which wasn't exactly a lovely sight. Functional but plain, the boxy galley terminated at one small window, affording barely a glance at the beautiful environs just beyond. Recognizing this problem, the owners called in an architect, asking him to open up the kitchen and make it more suitable for their informal lifestyle.

The first thing the architect did was remove the wall between the refrigerator and the foyer, separating each space with an oval island topped in granite. To keep the view from the living room unencumbered, he used a column to support the ceiling and then sheathed it in wood veneer for a seamless look. The same wood tone—maple stained to resemble pearwood—was chosen for the cabinets while unstained maple was installed on the floors. In altering the layout, the architect discovered a jumble of pipes and electrical lines hiding within the ceiling, so again he came up with a clever solution. Rather than impede his vision for a wide-open kitchen, he devised a free-form soffit in two levels that not only conceals the utilities but also adds a decorative element to the overall composition.

CLOCKWISE FROM TOP LEFT, BEFORE Low ceilings and minimal square footage made this dated kitchen a prime candidate for remodeling; Even with a private garden just outside, this insular kitchen could not salve the owners' desire for more interaction with the outdoors; For a couple that frequently hosts parties in their home, this limited amount of storage and serving space simply didn't fit the bill.

OPPOSITE, AFTER Warm wood tones and cool stainless steel work in perfect unison in this fresh, modern kitchen, creating a vivid interplay with the scenic natural surroundings.

Clever storage solutions make a kitchen more functional.

ABOVE RIGHT, AFTER Pouring gracefully into adjoining living areas, this kitchen reflects the casual attitude of its owners, who often open their home for entertaining.

OPPOSITE, AFTER The only thing better than abundant storage is abundant storage that melds seamlessly into the overall design, such as this hideaway pantry that poses no visual distractions or physical obstructions.

CASE STUDY: A Whole House Redone

Move or remodel—that was the choice facing the owners of this home. A young professional couple with small children, they needed more space for their growing family. With real estate values on the rise in their neighborhood, they found that a whole-house renovation, while expensive, was ultimately more cost-effective than moving and starting from scratch.

Problems: The Kitchen
TOO SMALL >> NO ACCESS TO POOL AREA >> LOW CEILING >> NO CHARACTER

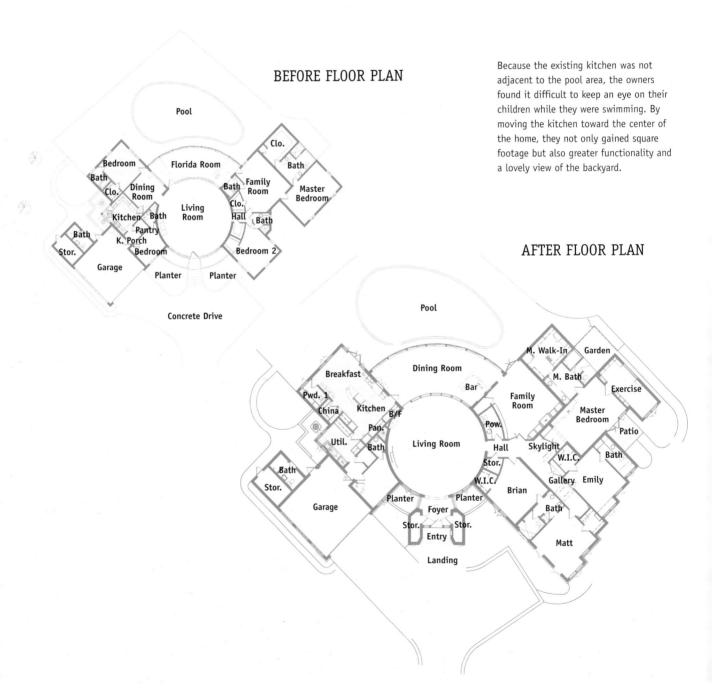

BEFORE FLOOR PLAN

Because the existing kitchen was not adjacent to the pool area, the owners found it difficult to keep an eye on their children while they were swimming. By moving the kitchen toward the center of the home, they not only gained square footage but also greater functionality and a lovely view of the backyard.

AFTER FLOOR PLAN

RIGHT, BEFORE Outdated appliances and minimal counter space made this galley-sized kitchen less than efficient, especially when entertaining.

BELOW, AFTER Using space formerly occupied by the dining room and a small bedroom, the kitchen was relocated to a more desirable spot in the home. By removing the bottom chord of the trusses, plans were implemented to fashion a tray ceiling that visually lifted the room and made it feel more open. Warmth was brought to the kitchen by installing handsome cherry wood cabinets.

ABOVE, AFTER After lining the backsplash area with vivid blue glass tiles, the homeowner took it one step further by coating the walls in a rich shade of azure. Balanced against the darkness of the wood and the natural tones of the garden outside, the color brings a sense of life and levity that the whole family enjoys.

OPPOSITE, AFTER Gleaming stainless steel appliances, including a handy wine cooler, set the theme for the rest of the metallic tones in the kitchen.

CHAPTER TWO:
Living Spaces

Family living spaces are the rooms where we spend the most time, so it's no surprise that they're magnets for just about everything. We kick up our feet to relax or watch TV, and suddenly the coffee table disappears beneath magazines, remote controls, and last night's homework. Nobody wants to spruce up when it's much more comfortable just to unwind, so gradually, over the years, family rooms and media rooms become less and less user-friendly. They're often the first rooms in need of renovation, but the last to actually be renovated. And it's not uncommon to see them swimming in gadgets.

In today's average living space, you might find a television, a stereo system, a DVD player, a satellite receiver, a TiVO recorder, surround-sound speakers, an MP3 player, a video game console, and a laptop computer. And somehow, within this mess of technology, people are also supposed to find room for eating, reading, napping, and enjoying each other's company!

So how can renovation address all these needs? The most obvious answer is space-planning. By carving out plenty of storage space and determining the most efficient layout for multiple activities, a thoughtful living space remodel can effectively beautify the room, modernize it, and guarantee flexibility for years to come.

ABOVE, AFTER Who wouldn't enjoy a spot of tea in this quiet reading nook? A perfect place to slow down and gather your thoughts, it offers a softer, more feminine take on a traditional library.

OPPOSITE, AFTER Inspired by a grand exterior staircase in Italy, this imposing cast keystone mantel recalls the romance and dignity of Old World Europe—exactly the mood that the owners of this Mediterranean-style villa were hoping to capture.

Using Drywall to Make Creative Changes

Originally designed in 1976, this contemporary-style house had a shed roof and 2,700 square feet (251 sq m) of living space. Since then, the owners have become empty-nesters, and their spatial requirements and lifestyle have changed considerably. They spend much of their leisure time in the family room, watching TV, visiting with grand-children, and simply enjoying the patio view. And though they were comfortable with the initial layout, they longed for a more modern space where the colors were lighter and brighter and the television didn't seem so overpowering.

The family room had a sloping ceiling covered in tongue-and-groove cedar, a plywood veneer soffit that was open at the top for lighting, and an 8' (2.4 m) sliding glass door

that led to the pool area outside. It also had a massive big-screen TV that the owners were looking to replace. After seeing some initial sketches from the architect, the owners were ultimately convinced to keep the television and rework the rest of the room. Rather than spend the money on a new TV, they elected to pay for a striking renovation.

First to go was the plywood soffit on one wall, replaced by a new drywall soffit on three walls. This addition concealed the air conditioner ducts and allowed for increased lighting, giving the room an almost gallery-like appearance. Each wall was then enhanced with drywall build-outs, creating special nooks for artwork and prized family photos. And finally, the TV was encased in a storage-rich wall unit and the entire space was freshly painted. Receding walls got a darker tone; protruding elements were coated in lighter shades.

In the end, relatively small changes made the family room feel like a brand new space. And because most of the new construction involved inexpensive drywall (used creatively), costs were kept to a minimum.

ABOVE LEFT, BEFORE An outdated paneled ceiling and large television overpowered this room, making it feel darker and smaller than it really was.

ABOVE RIGHT, BEFORE The homeowners' love of artwork and photography seemed a natural starting point for the redesign.

OPPOSITE, AFTER To stress the newfound fluidity of the family room (and save the owners from banging their shins), the original square coffee table was replaced with a custom-designed rounded one.

ABOVE, AFTER Encased in a built-in wall unit, the big-screen TV now seems less of an intrusive object and more of an organic component. The soffit repeats the style of the media cabinet, creating a unifying look throughout the room.

TOP RIGHT, BEFORE Though the initial floor plan was functional, it had not kept up with the family's changing needs and lifestyle. As a result, it needed a little tweaking.

BOTTOM RIGHT, AFTER The new floor plan incorporated significantly more display space for the owners' art collection as well as a sculptured wall for added interest.

FLOOR PLAN BEFORE

FLOOR PLAN AFTER

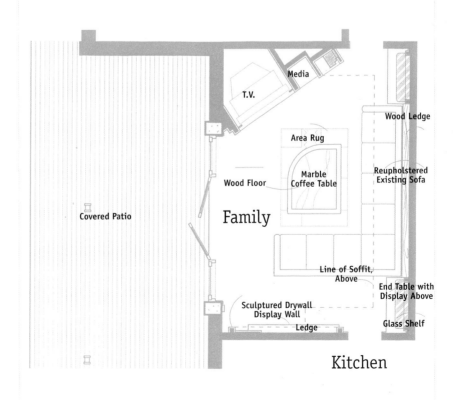

Transforming a Bland Hallway into a Vibrant Art Gallery

Even the most utilitarian spaces in a home can benefit from a refresher, as was the case with this dark and lifeless hallway. Lacking any real character or definition, it served as a connection between two children's bedrooms but offered little else in the way of form or function. What's worse, it was quite narrow—just a few feet wide—and broken up with an arching header that actually made the space feel smaller. The homeowners, hoping to enlarge the hallway and make it more open and cheerful, gave the architect free reign with design but advised him that they weren't willing to sacrifice square footage in other rooms to make the hallway wider.

He responded with a clever solution, first removing the header to open up the ceiling and then utilizing dead space between wall studs to create the illusion of depth. The drywall was then doubled up for added visual thickness, with deco-style sculptural build-outs crafted near the ceiling. Each recess was painted a rich shade of blue and then adorned with an African mask from the owners' collection. Crowned by mini spotlights within the recess and ocean blue sconces perched high above on two build-outs, the newly fashioned wall offers not only added space and increased illumination but also high-impact drama and a showplace for cherished artwork.

> *Even the most utilitarian spaces in a home can bring benefit from a refresher.*

LEFT, BEFORE Not even mirrors could make this cramped hallway feel larger, and the dull white walls detracted from it as well.

OPPOSITE, AFTER A soft neutral palette punctuated by bold blue accents brings this hallway into modern times, making it feel fresh, lively, and more livable.

Creating a Dramatic Entry with Open Stairs

As part of a whole house renovation, the owners of this lackluster foyer decided to add some oomph to their main entry area, completely re-envisioning the space and updating every inch. Their original staircase already served as a focal point because of its size and location, but it fell short of making a statement because it was dark, narrow, and poorly proportioned. Covered in worn carpet and boxed in by a low ceiling, it simply didn't feel contemporary, so a major overhaul was needed.

The architect began the transformation by looking for ways to open up the entire foyer, first removing a structural wall and then replacing it with a steel I-beam. Surprisingly enamored with the strong, industrial style of the beam, he allowed it to remain exposed and eventually set the tone of the design. For the new staircase, he chose steel tube supports painted in a royal burgundy color, both for drama and for a punch of color. He then capped the supports with thick maple stair treads—hefty slabs of smooth wood that appear to float weightlessly toward the second floor.

Newly created space behind the staircase serves as a cozy alcove for displaying artwork and greeting visitors. It also serves as an open and inviting transitional area between other rooms, which the owners find especially valuable for entertaining.

LEFT, BEFORE There's virtually nothing appealing about this dated entry area. Even the floor was begging to be replaced.

OPPOSITE, AFTER Light and airy, with a clean, neutral palette, the new foyer has a modern, ethereal quality that will serve the owners for decades to come.

OPPOSITE INSET, AFTER Drywall build-outs and recesses form interesting nooks where artwork can be beautifully showcased, especially when illuminated with dramatic lighting.

With good design, a foyer can serve as more than just an entryway.

Toning Down a Themed Design

Sometimes a homeowner places a highly personal stamp on a house that perfectly suits his or her tastes but does absolutely nothing for the next occupant. It could be bold paint colors or overly "period" light fixtures, or in the case of this living room, a very stylized fireplace. The previous owner's love of desert-inspired design resulted in a curved earthen mantel that, while attractive in its own right, was much more at home in an adobe dwelling than a sleek contemporary. To compound matters, the fireplace—tall and sinewy—served to elongate the already lofty living room, making it feel like a shoebox standing on end.

In addressing this problem, the architect crafted an asymmetrical chimney surround that was wider than it was tall. To further enhance the illusion of width, he designed the granite mantel to span all the way to the far wall of the living room, where a diagonal niche was added for visual interest and a punch of color. The marble hearth was also fashioned in an asymmetrical shape and positioned to appear as if it's floating, making it a focal point of the composition and a very striking example of contemporary style. It also stretches from wall to wall, bringing a newfound sense of proportion to this revamped space.

LEFT, BEFORE Blatantly themed rooms, such as this Southwestern living space complete with an Anasazi-style ladder, retain their relevance and desirability for only a short amount of time.

OPPOSITE, AFTER A black area rug helps to ground this lofty space, making it feel more intimate. Colorful furnishings and artwork infuse it with vitality while still allowing the room to remain relatively neutral.

Enlivening a Space with Appropriate Lighting

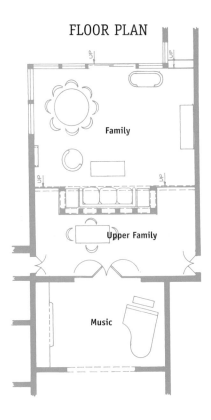

Advice from the Architect...

In important spaces, such as living rooms, family rooms, and kitchens, I usually try to have at least three different sources of light, each independently switched on dimmers. A decorative curved rail light with multiple low-voltage heads allows the flexibility to highlight artwork and also provide mood lighting. Low voltage or line voltage lights placed in drywall build-outs serve as perfect accent illumination. And xenon uplighting, which consists of a flexible plastic track with small bulbs, can be spaced at any interval for different effects. It seems to make the walls and ceiling float, and creates a very sexy atmosphere at night. If I'm working on a tight budget, I'll sometimes use rope lights instead of xenon. They're very inexpensive but they create the same nice glow.

OPPOSITE RIGHT, AFTER By reinforcing existing beams, the columns could be removed and a lovely view of the pool and garden became visible from all angles. The infusion of sunlight and installation of new light fixtures made the room instantly brighter.

OPPOSITE BOTTOM, BEFORE Already graced with copious natural light and a beautiful view, this bare living room was a blank canvas just waiting to be embellished.

RIGHT BOTTOM, BEFORE A row of columns restricted possibilities in this multiuse family room, making the space feel small, dark, and inefficient.

RIGHT TOP, AFTER Rather than opt for bold colors or busy patterns, the rich texture of the wood and the dramatic flair of the accent lighting was allowed to subtly highlight the bold statement made by this media wall.

BELOW By taking note of how the owners used these rooms on a daily basis, the architect determined the most effective flow and layout.

FLOOR PLAN

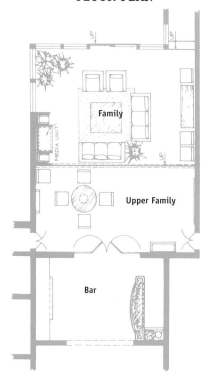

Creating More Storage in a Beautiful Way

The owners of this home needed additional space to display their artwork and store family photos, but they couldn't agree on what style the new design scheme should follow. The husband's taste ran toward the traditional, so he requested that the home's original columns be retained. The wife, on the other hand, had her sights set on a more contemporary look with clean lines, minimal fuss, and maple cabinetry. Ultimately, both of their desires were met through a clever mingling of both old and new.

The columns remained in place, but around them sprouted three walls of highly functional maple cabinets. One section conceals the couple's audio equipment. Another hides a large cold air return vent behind a decorative wooden grill. And along the top of both runs a length of *black absolute* granite that offers a stain resistant surface for flowers or drinks. Still other components of the cabinetry provide space for displaying photos or artwork, and, at the opposite end of the room, the centerpiece of the main unit is a big screen TV.

By building all the cabinets from maple, the look remains clean and consistent throughout the room, allowing each of the homeowner's distinct tastes to shine through.

TOP BELOW, BEFORE All eyes are drawn to the giant black television in this long, narrow room, where family photos and artwork are relegated to wherever they can fit.

BOTTOM BELOW, AFTER Designed to mirror the cabinets on the opposite end of the room, this shelving unit provides ample space for storage and display.

ABOVE, AFTER The newly coffered ceiling offers a decorative solution to concealing utilities while the maple wall unit artfully masks the oversized television.

RIGHT, BEFORE The only feature of interest in this empty end of the living room was the pair of columns marking the entryway.

CASE STUDY: A Whole House Redone

Initially this home had no foyer, so guests plopped awkwardly into the main living area, making it feel exposed and too wide open. With a newly renovated grand Mediterranean-style entry, this room instantly became a more sheltered space for family gatherings. "Now, as soon as you walk in you see the view to the garden," the architect says, "but the area around the fireplace still feels buffered and intimate."

Problems: Living Room
OBTRUSIVE A/C GRILLS >> DISJOINTED FURNITURE LAYOUT >> LACK OF WARMTH >> DATED DETAILS

BEFORE FLOOR PLAN

AFTER FLOOR PLAN

RIGHT, BEFORE Can a room be too large for its own good? Yes, as this free-floating jumble of furniture proves. More like a dance hall than a cozy spot for conversation, this sprawling living room suffered from inefficient use of square footage.

BELOW, AFTER While this unique circular room underwent almost no major structural changes, it was completely transformed with a few minor aesthetic tweaks and a fresh new layout. The furniture was positioned in a more close and comfortable manner, while the walls were given new life with a creamy faux finish. The band of textured paint above the brick line emphasizes the dramatic shape of the room, while also infusing the space with warmth.

CHAPTER THREE:
Dining Rooms and Gathering Spaces

Human beings have been sitting down to share food
and drink since the beginning of time, so it's no surprise that dining rooms and other intimate gathering spaces are still essential components of every modern home. Often frequented during evening hours, these rooms sometimes take on a dramatic quality not found in the rest of the house, with rich colors and intense textures given free reign to entice and allure. At their heart, they usually have a table, be it formal or informal, large or small, and of course, comfortable seating is essential. Another desirable feature in a dining area is close proximity to the kitchen, though this is less so if the room is primarily used for enjoying wine and spirits. In that case, a nearby bar or wine vault is preferable, or for some, even a humidor.

To make a dining or drinking space most conducive to good conversation, it's smart to illuminate it with at least two kinds of lighting. Utilitarian lights overhead allow guest to see and enjoy their food while ambient light helps to spark the mood and make everyone feel at ease. Candlelight—one variety of ambient light—is a must-have in any gathering space because it offers instant atmosphere, especially when bringing a soft glow to fresh flowers or glistening silverware.

TOP LEFT, AFTER A sophisticated retreat for any gentleman, this swank alcove brings new meaning to the idea of "corner bar." Stocked with fine liquors, comfy seats, and a nearby pool table, it offers an ideal haven for the man of the house.

OPPOSITE TOP LEFT, BEFORE This is a man's world. That's what the sports posters, cozy leather chairs, and dated decor say about this good-time bar area.

OPPOSITE TOP RIGHT, BEFORE A long, flat ceiling did nothing to invigorate this aging living room, where even natural light didn't lift the somber mood.

OPPOSITE BOTTOM, AFTER Reminiscent of a majestic grand hall in a medieval castle, this sumptuous dining room reflects the owners' love of exquisite natural materials, rich color, and sharing their home with friends.

Discovering Special Structure beneath Dropped Ceilings

Sometimes, after living in a house for a while, you discover that it just doesn't function in the way that you had hoped. The galley kitchen, which initially seemed so efficient, now feels impossibly small. The expansive master bath, which once looked so inviting, now reveals itself as a cavern of constant cleaning. And the casually sprawling living room, thought to be the heart of the home, turns out to be not so useful when it robs you of a convenient dining area. The latter was the quandary facing these homeowners, who longed for a simple eating space instead of a long and lingering living room. Consulting with an architect, they asked him to steal some square footage from one area and use it to carve out another, but what he delivered was so much more.

Removing the bottom chord of the ceiling trusses, he lifted the ceiling dramatically, opening up the living room to light and life. The trusses were held in place with collar ties and then enveloped in an attractive wood. Then, borrowing a few feet from the bedroom, the architect was able to open up the floor plan, and through careful space planning, he reserved one corner of the living room for a pleasant dining area. With the addition of colorful artwork and a delicate chandelier hanging overhead, the space became a delightful gathering spot for family meals and the house took on a lighter, more playful feel.

SITE & SECOND FLOOR PLAN BEFORE

SITE & SECOND FLOOR PLAN AFTER

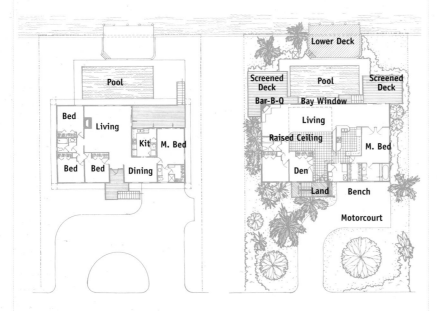

LEFT For this renovation, the footprint of the home basically stayed the same but the interior walls underwent drastic changes.

OPPOSITE, AFTER Soaring to new heights, this combination living and dining room is a cozy, flexible space that can easily switch personalities from day to night.

Raising the Roof with Coffered Details

With its sleek wall of glass block and stair-stepped soffits around the ceiling, this cozy dining room did have unique character in its original condition. Unfortunately, because it rested two steps up from the adjoining room, it also had an uncomfortably low ceiling and a stifling sense of enclosure. Recognizing this, the owners were interested in opening up the space and creating a greater connection to the adjacent foyer, so they tapped an architect for the job. Right away, he looked to the ceiling for greater possibilities.

By removing the drywall underneath the trusses and resheathing their sides with new sheetrock, he was able to construct an overhead grid with different-sized squares, creating the illusion of a raised ceiling. Within the grid, he placed delicate low-voltage lights for inconspicuous illumination, flooding the room with a warm radiance. Just below, he crafted a new dining room table, fashioning two rusted steel arches (coated in polyurethane) as the base and holding them together with two polished aluminum fins. The fins echo the shape of the new window and new foyer console—graceful curves that signal the renewed sense of softness in this freshly revamped room.

ABOVE, BEFORE Very Art Deco in style and feel, this vintage dining room did have one feature that the owners loved—a gorgeous herringbone wood floor.

OPPOSITE, AFTER The lattice grid in the new window is mirrored by an identical design in the new foyer console, allowing guests to see into the entryway while dining.

Adding Warmth with Wood Cabinets

Sometimes all a room needs is subtle tweaking to make it shine. That was the case with this largely agreeable dining room, where the owners gathered frequently with family and friends. A massive mirror swallowed up one entire wall, robbing the space of any color or dimension, while a row of white Formica cabinets seemed to exude a sense of blandness and fatigue. Even so, the room overlooked a stunning trio of garden windows, and the floor—a clean collection of marble squares—gave off just the right amount of elegance. What was missing, the owners' architect determined, was the richness of wood.

Drawing inspiration from the home's kitchen cabinets, he chose the same materials for the dining room buffet, covering it in golden teak and exuberant red sapele pommele. Just above, he scaled down the large mirror, framing a smaller looking glass in a wooden frame and creating recesses on either side for displaying artwork. To increase the room's connection to the rest of the house, the architect removed the wall to the kitchen and installed sliding, bi-parting doors that serve as a visual link between the two spaces, allowing the dining room to spill freely into other living areas.

ABOVE, BEFORE Just like flat soda, all the fizz was gone from this nondescript dining room, though the owners hoped it could be enlivened.

OPPOSITE, AFTER Contemporary artwork brings color and vitality to the room, making the original chairs and table seem newly interesting and purposeful.

CASE STUDY: A Whole House Redone

Since the old dining room was sacrificed in the name of a larger kitchen, the new dining room was shuffled to a lackluster exterior porch. Directly adjacent to the pool area, this exterior porch had everything in the way of location but nothing in the way of style, making it a perfect candidate for a minor remodel.

Problems: Dining Room
INSUFFICIENT LIGHTING >> UNATTRACTIVE SLIDING DOORS >> LACK OF TEXTURE AND WARMTH >> OBSTRUCTIVE WINDOW FRAMES

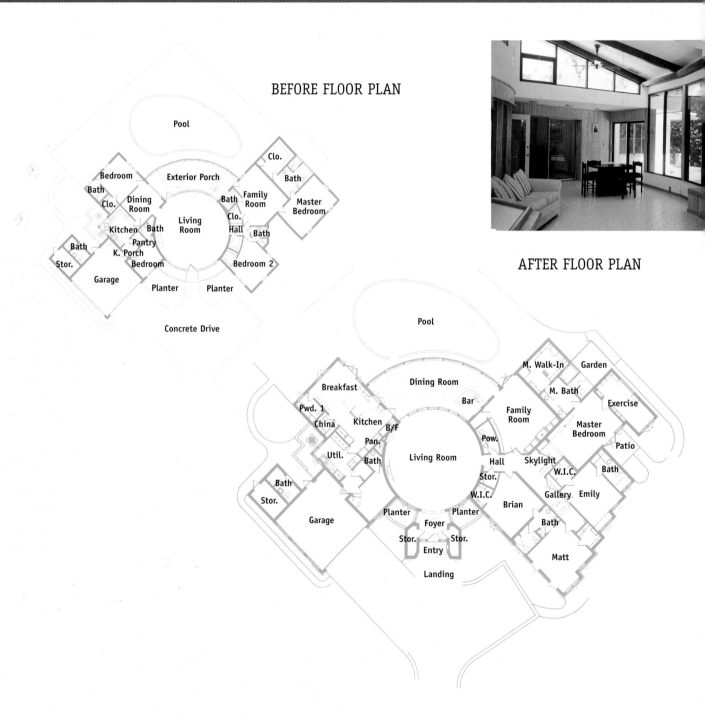

BEFORE FLOOR PLAN

AFTER FLOOR PLAN

OPPOSITE, BEFORE The term "wasted space" most certainly applied to this former exterior porch, where the only distinguishing characteristics were an odd little bench and a blank expanse of floor.

RIGHT, AFTER Sometimes all a room needs is a subtle facelift. Making the window frames sleeker and less noticeable paved the way for a lovely, unimpeded view of the pool. The space was also freshened up by installing a new stone floor that added drama by framing delicate sconces with silky taupe draperies.

BELOW, AFTER An eye-catching chandelier suspended from the ceiling high above complements the soaring roofline. Choosing understated yet properly scaled furnishings and accessories ensured that the room's finer points would not go unnoticed. "It's all about balance," says the architect.

CASE STUDY: A Whole House Redone

Problems: The Bar
UGLY DECOR >> OUTDATED FIXTURE >> LACK OF STORAGE SPACE

TOP LEFT, BEFORE Located at the opposite end of the exterior porch, this bar area had the potential to be an attractive gathering spot but its 1970s decor left it feeling cold and uninviting.

BELOW, AFTER Soft, lighthearted fabrics and flirty barstools infuse this space with a punch of personality, making it seem welcoming for "patrons" of all ages. Raised moldings add a visual thrill to the front of the bar, complementing the handsome paneled cabinets in the rear.

OPPOSITE, AFTER Like the dining room, this bar needed only minor changes to become more desirable. By leaving the plumbing fixtures in the same place, additional resources could be devoted to warm cherry wood cabinetry, easy-care granite countertops, and a large built-in wine rack.

CHAPTER FOUR:
Sleeping Spaces

Deny someone a good night's rest, and he's sure to be cranky come morning. But rob him of sleep over a period of time—days, months, even years—and the effect of chronic insomnia will indelibly mark his personality for the worse. No doubt about it, sleep is absolutely vital to the healthy working of a human body, so it makes perfect sense that we should strive to create idyllic sleeping environments. Throughout history, several innovations have made bedrooms more amenable, including the ability to regulate temperature and light on a consistent basis. Advents in mattress design, textiles, pillows, and even pajamas have also helped people sleep more soundly. But how much effect do architecture and design have on restfulness?

Studies show that certain colors do in fact calm the nerves, priming people for sleep. Passive and neutral tones of green, blue, purple, taupe, and gray have all proven to be good choices for bedrooms, though some find electric red or shocking orange to be just as desirable. As with all design, personal choice is the deciding factor, and what soothes one person may be jarring to another. But there is some evidence that the harmony of one's surroundings can strongly impact emotions, mindset, and certainly health.

Hospital patients have been known to recover more quickly when they're able to view nature from their beds. And all of us, regardless of our knowledge of architecture, have all felt the positive energy of a comfortable room versus the nagging anxiety of a confined or windowless space. Our spirits soar and unwind in beautiful places, sink and tense up in those that feel ugly. So yes, architecture does contribute to restfulness—on a deeply innate, powerful level that affects us every single night.

Warm wood tones give bedrooms an air of coziness.

ABOVE, BEFORE This was actually a pleasant room with a lot of personality but it really needed some architectural TLC and deft decorating touches to make it sing.

OPPOSITE, AFTER With the addition of sconces and a freshly cleaned beamed ceiling, the whole room has a fresher, brighter look—all without compromising its original style.

Promoting Restfulness with a Raised Ceiling

Stately design was the hallmark of this 1930s Mediterranean-style home, where the owners hoped to modernize without making major modifications. A young couple with a teenage daughter, they wanted to enhance their casual lifestyle by creating a lighter, airier feeling in their house and increasing the visual flow to the outdoors, but they didn't want to forfeit the integrity of the home's vintage style. As part of a large-scale rehab, their master bedroom received a careful facelift in which unattractive elements were concealed and new details were added to complement the architecture. And the ceiling, which became the highlight of the room, was raised to soaring new heights.

By removing the bottom chord of the trusses and restructuring the top chords, the ceiling was lifted significantly and then trimmed out in properly scaled molding, part of which held cove lighting. The added height and light helped to create an elegant and tranquil setting in the bedroom. Underfoot, well-worn carpeting was replaced with wood floors in a mahogany herringbone pattern while on the walls, a fresh coat of paint and handsome new light sconces filled the space with renewed beauty. As an added bonus, the architect was able to redistribute a large dressing room into a his-and-hers walk-in closet, creating the perfect union of form and function.

ABOVE, BEFORE A plethora of vents and outlets brought visual clutter to this otherwise bare bedroom, causing the space to feel broken up and busy.

OPPOSITE, AFTER With its newly raised ceiling and soft palette of taupes, pinks, and soothing greens, this bedroom is a peaceful retreat that feels warmly enveloped by the garden outside.

Remodeling a Child's Bedroom for Sweet Dreams

A child's bedroom is always evolving, changing with the needs and tastes of its occupant. And so was the case with this growing boy's remodeled space. Originally just a small room with a simple dresser and a car-shaped bed, it worked fine while the child was still young. But as he matured, he literally outgrew it. The bed became too small. The desk, with its child-size drawers, soon overflowed with clothes and toys. And the closet, while certainly expansive, was not outfitted in a way that allowed efficient storage or easy access.

The architect resolved this problem by first expanding the size and height of the room, borrowing space from the family room below. Although a girder truss proved to be an obstacle and the flat roof of the family room was higher than the floor of the bedroom, he came up with an ingenious plan to create three separate levels. The lower level, equal in height to the adjoining hallway, became the boy's study. Two steps up, the second level housed his bed. And the third level, three steps up, was morphed into a play area.

To alleviate the lack of height in the middle level, the architect removed the drywall in the existing ceiling, exposing a lofty series of beams. He then sheathed the structural wood in the same veneer as that used on the bed, desk, and casework, creating a harmonic, airy space that would suit a person of any age.

ABOVE LEFT, BEFORE Dark brown carpeting and tan walls did little to enhance the desirability of this bedroom, much less make it conducive to playtime.

OPPOSITE, AFTER Sleek, modern light fixtures and contemporary-style carpeting complement the pale tone of the woodwork, giving this second-floor bedroom a light, airy, treehouse feel.

Adding Interest by Incorporating Build-Outs

A drab shoebox—that's the best way to describe this bedroom in its "before" state. Riddled with visually obtrusive air conditioning vents, and dressed in dreary shades of timeworn tan, it was plain vanilla and more than ready for a makeover. As part of a whole-house renovation, the owners wanted it to be consistent with the rest of the home's detailing, which was largely contemporary. But they also hoped it could have special character of its own. Guided by this request, the architect fashioned layer upon layer of drywall build-outs, creating a wealth of dimension for very little money. Closing up a small window that flooded the room with hot afternoon sun, he replaced it with a sweeping headboard that spans the entire length of one wall. Almost like a piece of sculpture, the headboard not only keeps pillows in place but also provides a venue for showcasing artwork. Petite spotlights fill each niche, draping the room in diffused light while a specially designed valance over the patio doors hides a convenient remote control shade.

Plants and natural sunlight fill a bedroom with warmth and energy.

Advice from the Architect...

I always know what I want the outside of a home to look like after the renovation, but I never show my clients an exterior plan until the inside layout is done and approved. If I present the elevations first, the owners are often reluctant to make changes to the floor plan for fear that the façade I designed (and that they fell in love with) will have to be changed. I know I can make anything look like anything, especially on an exterior façade, so I hold off on that until the end to make sure the layout is perfect first. That way the client is happy all around.

OPPOSITE, BEFORE A plain old rectangular space with no personality, this bedroom failed to take advantage of the lush garden environs just beyond.

ABOVE, AFTER Awash in crisp tones of white, this dramatically renovated bedroom is now a quiet whisper of a space, easily spilling onto the veranda outside and providing a soothing oasis for its owners.

CASE STUDY: A Whole House Redone

Two generous new additions allowed for expansion of the master bedroom and definition of a whole wing of the house to be designed for the three children's bedrooms. In changing the overall footprint of the home, a private patio was created off of the master suite, as well as private bathrooms for the kids.

Problems: The Master Bedroom
NO PRIVACY FROM THE HALLWAY >> NO SPACE FOR A TREADMILL >> BLAND, BOXY DESIGN

BEFORE FLOOR PLAN

AFTER FLOOR PLAN

RIGHT, BEFORE Just a plain, boxy space with no interesting features—that's what this master bedroom looked like before renovation. It had no architectural detail and no real sense of style.

ABOVE, AFTER The lady of the house insisted that her husband's treadmill find a new home outside of the master bedroom, so an efficient nook was fashioned in the narrowest of spaces. In barely 160 square feet (15 sq m) exists a well-appointed office, handsome bookshelves, and a small exercise area.

BOTTOM RIGHT, AFTER The new layout demanded that the kids walk past the parents' room to reach their own, but a clever vestibule just outside the master suite provides an added layer of privacy. To welcome in sunlight but not a lot of heat, the architect also installed a 2' x 2' (0.6 x 0.6 m) skylight with a sweeping 4' x 4' (1.2 x 1.2 m) well.

CASE STUDY: A Whole House Redone

Problems: The Kids' Bedroom
LACK OF STORAGE SPACE >> OUTGROWN DECOR >> INSUFFICIENT LIGHTING >> NO CHARACTER

RIGHT, BEFORE Size-wise, this room was plenty big for a growing young girl, but it lacked sufficient storage or organization to really be a desirable space.

BELOW, AFTER Redesigned from top to bottom, this spring-colored bedroom uses layers of interesting textures and charming touches that would enchant any young princess. "It's sweet but sophisticated, with basic decor elements able to withstand many years of changing tastes."

LEFT, BEFORE The bare walls and makeshift furniture of this bedroom didn't suit the vibrant personality of the middle-schooler who slept there, so a newly imagined decor was long overdue.

ABOVE, AFTER After coating one wall in a richly textured faux finish and topping the windows with tailored valances, Barry added further warmth and utility by installing wooden built-ins in two corners.

CHAPTER FIVE:
Bathrooms

We've come a long way in the history of bathrooms, from the good green earth to polite chamber pots to rustic outhouses to our current state of luxury, indoor plumbing. But in recent years, bathrooms have become even more splendid. Now serving as lavish bathing and primping facilities that often rival professional spas, they entice you to linger and pamper yourself, to escape from the world in a fluff of bubbles or a cloud of steam. For many, they also act as impromptu dressing rooms, allowing people to preen in front of a mirror while getting their lipstick or necktie or hairline just right.

Bathrooms are an integral part of our lives, so it's only logical that we would instill them with such importance. They are places of rejuvenation and retreat (just ask any mother), so we need them to be functional, inviting, and most importantly comfortable. In designing the ultimate bathroom, tastes and needs obviously take precedent, but we can all agree on common elements—a soothing shower or bathtub, a functioning toilet, and a refreshing sink. Anything else is just a bonus.

ABOVE, BEFORE Compact but practical, this bathroom's biggest fault was its grimy old shower and overpowering vanity.

LEFT, AFTER Clean and simple is the name of the game in this modest space, where translucent glass and marble set on the diagonal help to broaden the room and make it feel less weighty.

OPPOSITE, AFTER A luminous art glass bowl serves as a gleaming centerpiece in this warm envelope of a powder room, filling the largely neutral space with a wink of bold color.

Adding Style with Natural Wood and Stone

Elegance was the word of the day when the owners of this tired bathroom set out to remodel it. Reserving the space primarily for guests, they wanted it to be clean and simple but with a subtle hint of refinement. They also demanded that the original footprint not be changed, so the architect was really put to the test. To meet their requirements, he worked within the existing layout, finding creative ways to replace the worn sink and vanity with modern alternatives. He designed a curving vanity made from English sycamore, then topped it with an alluring glass bowl sink and marble countertop. Overhead, he repeated the convex shape on a striking light fixture, softly illuminating the area below and centering all attention on the sculptural quality of the sink. Just behind, in a slight recess, he placed a large mirror, hoping to fool the eye into thinking that the bathroom is larger than it actually is. To further enhance the space, he coated the walls in a soft shade of mauve—the same shade, in fact, as the quiet vein of pink marble used as an accent on the floor. When the project was complete, the owners were understandably bowled over.

LEFT, BEFORE Time had not been kind to this bathroom, leaving a dated pink sink, poorly placed vanity, and cumbersome ceiling-mounted water heater in its wake.

OPPOSITE, AFTER A raised ceiling and floating vanity bring this fabulous new powder room into the here and now.

Reviving Elegance with Contemporary Materials

Silver, gold, bronze, or copper—which tone do you prefer for your bathroom fixtures? The owners of this 1980s bathroom clearly had a passion for brass, using it to strike gold in nearly every inch of the space. With gold faucets, gold shower trim, gold towel holders, and even shiny brass bidet knobs, they likely had visions of luxury. But decades later, their theme just looked tired. They wound up seeking a modern makeover from an architect, asking him to update the space and make it flow naturally with the rest of the house. The layout was fine, he decided, but everything else would need to change.

After building out the sloped ceiling with soffits, giving the room an instant lift, he replaced the dated wallpaper with smooth white walls and marble tiles, and then plucked out the old shower. In its place, he installed a frameless glass unit that creates the illusion of added space, and crafted a convenient marble bench inside. Guided by the materials used in other rooms, he built the cabinets using maple and pearwood and even carved out a niche for a vanity seat. With a fresh new array of textures and contemporary fixtures, the bathroom is luxurious once again.

ABOVE, BEFORE Tacky feathered wallpaper casts a gray din over the entire bathroom, just crying out to be removed.

LEFT, AFTER Boldly veined marble surrounds the Jacuzzi tub, sparking a bit of elegance while still remaining within a neutral palette.

OPPOSITE, AFTER Rich in both storage and tone, this ultra-efficient vanity expresses the playful side of its owners' personalities through plucky sea-themed pulls and knobs.

Building Unity through Common Design Elements

Remodeling a home often reveals mysteries about its past, not to mention old design decisions that seem to have no basis in logic. When the owners of this modest powder room hired an architect to renovate it, they were surprised to learn that a space-stealing diagonal wall was not filled with wires and pipes as everyone suspected. Instead, it was just plain empty. A blessing as far as discoveries go, this dead area allowed the architect to make the room much larger than initially planned, taking it from modest to exceptional almost immediately.

Because the powder room rests directly adjacent to the family's media room and kitchen, his design was intended to borrow existing textures and colors from the main living areas. Pulling from the grid pattern of the media unit and wine rack, he created attractive storage compartments under the vanity for towels and other toiletries. He also trimmed out the mirror in the same rich wood tones used throughout the house, and chose a striking "broken" bronze sink as a focal point.

By carefully weaving a thread between the powder room and adjoining spaces, he not only produced a dazzling example of contemporary design but also developed a unified scheme that will serve the homeowners for many years.

FAR LEFT, BEFORE Busy wallpaper was the least of the problems in this blatantly early '80s powder room.

LEFT, BEFORE The disco era was alive and well in this odd-shaped bathroom, where space-age fixtures and smoky mirrors sent a definitely not-groovy message.

OPPOSITE, AFTER Guests are sure to appreciate the artful beauty of this uniquely renovated bathroom, especially the ragged edge granite slab that serves as a backdrop for the faucet.

Bathrooms, like kitchens, are easily dated by the choice of fixtures.

Borrowing Space to Enhance Functionality

Even for a powder room used primarily by guests, this tiny space was far from workable. Packed in a pint-sized footprint longer than it was wide, the room held a sink, a commode, and little else. Dark earth tones on the walls and floor only made it feel smaller, even with the bold reflection of an oversized mirror. To remedy the situation, the architect expanded the bathroom into an adjacent closet, enlarging it twofold. In doing so, he also outfitted the space with new cabinets, choosing English sycamore trimmed in rich travertine marble for an elegant look. He then covered the floor in a second shade of marble for contrast. Crown molding was added to the ceiling as well as trim molding just below, and an arched recess was crafted above the sink. Two sconces, matched to a parallel pendant fixture, were installed for utility lighting, though they also give the room a rich, lovely glow.

The new space, though still not large, efficiently takes advantage of every inch, forming a powder room that's welcoming for guests and delightful enough for everyday use.

LEFT, BEFORE Forced to make do in a cramped, ill-designed space, the owners of this wee powder room had to run a power cord all the way down the wall.

OPPOSITE, AFTER With a sculptural bowl sink and a small collection of vividly hued artwork, this bathroom has been transformed into a mini gallery.

Distinguishing a Bathroom
with Suspended Lighting

Chocolate-toned tiles and over-the-hill fixtures signaled a need for change in this 1970s bathroom, though the owners were insistent that the plumbing stay in the same location. Knowing that moving pipes greatly increases the costs during remodeling, they asked the architect to create impact in other ways. His first move, undeniably dramatic, was to flood the room with sunshine by installing skylights. He then built two cantilevered knee braces on the rear wall and used them to support a pair of contemporary pendant lights. Detailed with just a hint of blue, the striking fixtures echo the cobalt tiles used throughout the room, both around the sink and in the shower.

The sink itself—an elegant glass bowl—rests atop a slab of polished granite, which injects a subtle ribbon of neutral tones into the space. For added dimension, a small ledge was constructed behind the countertop, offering a convenient place for displaying flowers, soaps, or artwork. Just opposite, the frameless glass shower enclosure furthers the sophisticated style, adding to the open, spacious look of this freshly reworked and newly functional bathroom.

LEFT, BEFORE Inadequate lighting, dingy shower doors, and dark brown tiles gave this blah bathroom somewhat of a somber feel.

OPPOSITE, AFTER A simple palette of taupe and white gains greater interest with a hint of blue as an accent color. Large porcelain tiles also help to lighten and brighten the space.

Skylights, especially vented ones, are a welcome addition to any bathroom

Creating a "His and Hers" Look with Vintage Details

Many people have to share a bathroom with their spouse, so having separate facilities for both husband and wife is a luxury not lost on these homeowners. They were both relatively pleased with their respective rooms when they first considered renovating but they did hope an architect could solve a few small problems. The wife, happy to have plenty of vanity space, simply wanted to rearrange her windows to better accommodate a lovely view. And the husband, largely pleased with his existing sink, only desired updated cabinets. Both wanted a more modern decor.

Starting in the ladies bathroom, the architect removed one window and enlarged another, facing it opposite a massive mirror that reflects the bay outside. He then crafted arched openings above the shower and vanity—a nod to the home's Mediterranean architecture—and fashioned a gracious raised tub encased in taupe-colored marble. The marble was continued around most of the room, broken up only by the walnut cabinets and molding and tiny inlays of dark brown granite in the floor. Bold yet sophisticated, it gives this woman's bathroom a soothing, Old World spa feel.

In the gentleman's quarters, the mood is remarkably different. With a palette based in black and cobalt blue, the space centers around an eye-catching ceramic tile art piece, which the homeowner found and immediately became enamored with. So as not to steal the focus away from this image, the architect opted for streamlined cabinets and a sleek, simple layout. Iridescent tiles punctuate the design, along with cobalt blue sconces and the original black sink. And because the sink no longer contrasts with the rest of the bathroom, it now seems like a fine art piece in and of itself.

LEFT, BEFORE With no traditional vanity drawers and little storage, the homeowners were forced to keep most of their essentials in full display on the countertop.

OPPOSITE, AFTER Marble is always beautiful, but without the contrast of another texture, it would be cold and uninviting.

OPPOSITE INSET, BEFORE This very special vintage sink lost its prominence when surrounded by stark white cabinets and a lackluster design scheme.

OPPOSITE, AFTER Clean lines and crisp, manly colors infuse this gentleman's bathroom with a unique sense of style. Updated fixtures also make it more user-friendly.

BELOW, AFTER Arched build-outs and coffered ceilings help to soften the bathroom and make it feel more open and spacious. A glass-enclosed shower and graceful fixtures imbue it with an extra dash of sophistication.

Exploiting Angles for Maximum Impact

How do you accommodate a shower in a room shaped like a trapezoid? In this case, the architect decided to go with the flow. The only way he could make it fit was to place it on an angle, door and all, and then build everything else around it in a similarly skewed fashion. Using strongly linear zebra wood, he sliced the linen closet at a sharp angle, cutting through it with a "floating" stainless steel soffit that reflects light and makes the room feel larger. He also drew inspiration from the nearby ocean, laying blue glass tiles in both a matte and polished finish along the walls and floor and then painting the ceiling in a deep primary shade. By remaining open-minded, he was able to tackle a challenging problem with relative ease.

Contrasting textures, such as mood and metal, add impact to a bathroom

Advice from the Architect...

The most obvious element to avoid when remodeling is the "color of the year" syndrome. Thinking back to the work I've done, I can remember the blue-green year, the avocado gold year, the mauve year, and many more. To avoid using trendy colors, be creative with your combinations and be sure that they fit the personality of your home. My favorite trick is to look at a painting or print from a famous artist that my client admires—twentieth-century painter, Richard Diebenkorn, for example, or one of the masters such as Van Gogh, or Monet—and then use it as a color reference. These artists have been studying colors and how they work together for many years, so why reinvent the wheel? Pluck these colors from the canvas and put them onto your walls. The combinations will stand the test of time!

ABOVE, BEFORE A sad hodgepodge of outdated fixtures and heavily textured tile-work sent the owners of this small guest bathroom scrambling for a renovation.

OPPOSITE, AFTER The key to designing a room this dramatic is to keep the details relatively simple, which is why the architect chose clean-lined fixtures throughout.

ABOVE, BEFORE Like the teenager who used it, this bathroom was ready to grow up. Heavy striped wallpaper and old fixtures kept it from being as appealing as it could be.

LEFT, AFTER Electric aqua blue—the perfect color for a young girl's bathroom. The architect encouraged his client's daughter to choose the palette and then complemented it with clean-lined white cabinets, a uniquely shaped mirror, and plenty of storage.

RIGHT, AFTER With nowhere to go but up, the architect molded this bland space into a wow-worthy bathroom, creating a special arched alcove for the sink area. He allowed the palette to stay neutral, using crisp white tiles to form the easy-care wainscoting.

BELOW, BEFORE Nothing says "icky" like a depressing old bathroom with beat-up cabinets and absolutely no sense of style.

CASE STUDY: A Whole House Redone

Problems: The Master Bathroom
AWKWARD LAYOUT >> DATED DECOR >> LIMITED PRIVACY

TOP LEFT, BEFORE The basic design of this bathroom abounded with good ideas but the execution fell short, leaving assets such as the glass-walled shower not as attractive or useful as it could be.

BOTTOM LEFT, AFTER By moving the vanity across the room, a central corridor was created that allows easy access to the adjacent walk-in closet. The vanity itself became enriched storage by designing "his and hers" sink areas flanked by cherry wood cabinets.

ABOVE, AFTER To create a greater sense of privacy, the walls around the shower and water closet were beefed up and extended all the way to the ceiling. Acid-etched glass panels add an extra barrier as well as give the bathroom a spalike feel.

RIGHT, AFTER More than just a bathing station, this exceptional shower spills open to a private garden just outside. A delight for all the senses, it's further enhanced by the natural beauty of the bathroom's extensive marble work.

CASE STUDY: A Whole House Redone

Opposed to positioning a bathroom or closet at the end of a hallway, the center hall layout was reworked in this new addition. "I always try to create something visually appealing at the end of a vista," the architect says. This strategy produced two new private bathrooms, a relocated powder room, and a striking central gallery.

Problems: The Powder Room
TOO SMALL >>DATED DECOR >>POOR LIGHTING

BEFORE FLOOR PLAN

AFTER FLOOR PLAN

ABOVE, BEFORE What can you say about this pint-sized powder room? It's as minimal and compact as nearly every other basic bathroom in America. It serves its purpose just fine, but the aesthetics leave a lot to be desired.

RIGHT, AFTER In borrowing space from a former closet, a new sweeping layout was designed, complete with a separate water closet. The gently rounded cabinet is complemented by tumbled marble floors, crown molding, and richly elegant wall panels made from chocolate travertine marble.

CHAPTER SIX:
Outdoor Spaces

Nature renews us, filling us with hope for a new season or a cleansing rain, and we could not survive without it. Even within a sea of skyscrapers, the sight of a falling leaf or cool patch of grass is always a welcome respite. Surrounded by nature's bounty—in a verdant park or lush backyard—its power expands ten-fold, becoming more evident and more intoxicating to our spirits. And then we know, with this frenzied modern world spinning around us, that if we don't take time to smell the roses, life will simply not be as sweet.

That's why we build gardens. The outdoor spaces around our homes are vitally important to our daily experience, and the fact that we work so hard to improve our patios, yards, pools, and front entries is just proof of that. Environment matters. It's where we entertain friends and gather with family. It's what we see when we take in a beautiful view. And it's how we know that we're just one small part of the larger mystery. So go ahead, soak it up.

TOP LEFT, BEFORE As the outdoor recreation zone for a busy family with five children, this yard needed to serve many purposes and offer activities for all ages.

BOTTOM LEFT, BEFORE Though appealing in concept, the grass-roofed cabana felt isolated from the swimming area, so it was used infrequently.

BOTTOM RIGHT, BEFORE Despite having a tennis court and amoeba-shaped swimming pool, this backyard lacked a cohesive plan that would unify its amenities.

ABOVE, AFTER From beneath the gabled-end covered patio, guests can enjoy a meal, find shelter from the rain, or view the sculpture at the far end of the pool.

LEFT, AFTER Enlarged and reshaped to accommodate competitive lap swimming, the new pool offers a wide step area for relaxing and lounging. It also has a generous swim-out at the deep end, so family members can bask in the sun while being partly submerged.

ABOVE, AFTER A new cabana took shape at the southern end of the property, providing a changing room, towel storage, and eating area. Nearby, a raised hot tub overflows into a trickling waterfall, sending soothing sounds throughout the backyard.

Enhancing a Garden with the Soothing Sounds of Water

After redesigning this client's kitchen—an internal space that faced a somewhat shabby play area—the architect wanted to create a pleasant garden that could be viewed from inside. He had recently installed a large north-facing window to welcome in the joy of the morning light, so he felt compelled to justify it with a worthy vista. After removing all the grass from the play area, he started the transformation by constructing concrete benches and a small reflecting pond. Then, expanding on his initial idea for peace and tranquility, he designed a simple fountain that would allow the homeowners to hear the calming sound of falling water. Dispensed from a beam supported by concrete columns, the water trickled out, gently cascading over a concrete bridge underneath. Serene and relaxing, it was surrounded by a keystone patio deck, which was further enveloped by a lush border of trees and shrubs. In the end, the homeowners were not only impressed with the view from their kitchen but eager to enjoy their new meditation garden up close

ABOVE, BEFORE A nondescript side yard offered the owners little in the way of aesthetics or function, instead serving as a storage area for toys and supplies.

RIGHT, AFFTER Inspired by the Zen gardens of Asia, this placid outdoor room offers a quiet place to read, meditate, or simply soak up the beauty of the landscape. Tooled concrete benches embody the spirit of simple elegance.

Bringing Harmony to a Family Entertaining Area

Like a leaf blowing in the wind, this lackluster swimming pool seemed to be drifting all on its own, with no connection to the adjoining house. It did nothing to complement the stately architecture of the beautiful Mediterranean Revival home, and from a functional standpoint it offered very little in the way of amenities. To resolve this shortcoming, the architect constructed an outdoor eating area adjacent to the pool, drawing inspiration from the detailing of the house to create a weathered sense of timelessness.

A checkerboard pattern of glazed blue tile, so Mediterranean in flavor, was used to sheath the walls and countertop, while warm terracotta was used on the base of the bar and the floor. In the cooking area, a Y-shaped range hood was positioned against the wall, rising grandly above a row of wooden cabinets and just parallel to a pair of light fixtures covered in a rich patina. To tie everything together, the architect allowed the terracotta to ramble casually toward the pool, creating a keystone pattern on the deck and a cohesive visual signature. Wood chairs and benches, liberally placed throughout the yard, added an additional layer of unity, making the swimming area and the cooking cabana feel like one glorious outdoor retreat.

LEFT, BEFORE There's nothing wrong with this pool per se, but with no defined gathering area, it's not exactly a great place to mingle with friends.

OPPOSITE, AFTER Now this is a pool straight from paradise. Not only does the tilework seem richer and more inviting than the old brick but the new cabana is a beckoning haven with undeniable charm.

Meeting Building Codes with Ingenious Alternatives

One issue sure to arise during every renovation is how to deal with stringent building codes and still accomplish what you aim to do. For this exterior makeover, the local codes called for a 25′ (7.6 m) setback from the street, and because the house sat at exactly that distance, there was no room to expand forward. Pressed to come up with a clever solution, the architect found a loophole that allowed for a 3′ (0.9 m) roof overhang, so he built the entire façade around that flexibility. He designed a dimensional stucco build-out that varied from 4″ to 16″ (10 to 41 cm) deep and called it a dropped soffit, carefully articulating the line, depth, and character of the home's exterior without breaking the law. For added depth, he also angled the window walls, creating the illusion of even greater dimension.

Because the build-outs fall 1′ (0.3 m) short of the soffit, they appear to float gracefully in space. And because they rise 2′ (0.6 m) above the ground, the footprint of the home has technically remained the same and the new survey has not reflected an increase in square footage. This is all legal, of course, and exactly the kind of ingenuity you should expect from an experienced architect.

ABOVE, BEFORE Flat and featureless, this basic 1960s ranch house struggled to put its best face forward.

RIGHT, AFTER The front entry surround is stepped with stucco and punctuated by a snappy bright blue door. To echo the style of the build-outs, the door was adorned with thin strips of wooden battens.

LEFT, AFTER To have an efficient indoor kitchen is one thing, but a perfectly workable outdoor kitchen is like a dream come true. This mellow space, perfect for entertaining friends and family, is outfitted with everything you need for a night under the stars.

ABOVE, AFTER Transformed by a new roofline, hearty balustrades, and a stunning veranda addition, the revamped house now resembles an Old World villa with a fresh modern twist.

OPPOSITE TOP, BEFORE In its original state, this 1950s waterside home was a far cry from the Mediterranean villa its owners envisioned.

OPPOSITE BOTTOM, AFTER To complement their new façade, the owners of this freshened up contemporary installed a brick-bordered driveway and all new landscaping, using only plants that suited the home's scale and character.

Cooling a Hot Home with a New Veranda

This lovely home faces the southwest with a magnificent view of waterways. In the late afternoon the sun can be brutal, degrading furniture and carpeting in very short order, so the homeowners were desperate for a solution. Wanting to block the sun with an altered roofline and also transform their 1950s house into a Mediterranean-style villa, they hired an architect to overcome the challenge. His solution was to build a grand veranda. By generously raising the roof above the house and sloping it at the same angle, prevailing southeastern breezes were allowed to flow between the house and the new addition, providing the space with natural cooling. In adding this extra height, he could also design gracious arches supported by stucco columns, giving the owners the look they so desired. He opted to build the roof with heavy timbers encased in tongue-and-groove decking, giving the structure a bold yet rustic feel.

With construction of the veranda complete, the architect turned his attention to the pool area, installing a raised fountain sheathed in blue tile. He reshaped the pool and added a vast keystone deck that harmonized with the larger design, adding a decorative arched wall at one end. This not only offered privacy from the neighbors but also provided a discreet hiding place for the pool pump and filter.

ABOVE, The alluring waters of the bay spread out like a lush blue welcome mat at the foot of this newly inviting property. Colorful landscaping ringing the pool area makes it feel like a tropical paradise.

OPPOSITE, Careful attention to architectural detail allowed this veranda to sprout naturally from the original home, creating an illusion that it had been there all along.

Embracing the Mood with Color and Fun

It's a common sight in warm climates—the gargantuan screened room awkwardly hovering over a backyard pool. Good at keeping bugs at bay but bad at creating ambiance, cage-like enclosures are not exactly things of beauty, a fact that the owners of this home knew all too well. Their drab island dwelling was not only shrouded by a massive bug stopper, but its façade did little to entice the imagination. Plain and flat, with few interesting details, it didn't match the playful mood of its surroundings, a mellow vacation spot known for its beautiful beaches and resort atmosphere.

To dress up the pool area, the architect removed the screen and replaced it with gable-end versions that actually complement the architecture rather than detract from it. He also swapped the home's existing asphalt roof with clean-looking galvanized aluminum, and wrapped the painted plywood walls in horizontal siding. Covered staircases, reminiscent of the Victorian style so prevalent on the island, were added to each end of the house, both for convenience and visual interest, while vibrant shades of blue and magenta were chosen for the trimwork.

As the focal point in the pool area, the homeowner bucked the architect's recommendation of a lighthouse, instead choosing a big, bold tree trunk that had been carved into the shape of a woman. Lovingly referred to as "Big Bertha," the 8' (2.4 m) sculpture added an extra layer of fun and festivity to this newly lively backyard, serving as a whimsical focal point and a local landmark.

OPPOSITE, BEFORE Who wants to drop anchor at this dreary destination, an aging backyard bug cage with no visual appeal?

ABOVE, AFTER Brimming with verdant foliage, electric colors, and a fresh take on dated architecture, this feel-good oasis is a magnet for family and friends.

Welcoming Guests with a Grand New Entryway

With no real sense of entry, this house offered a not-so-enticing view of the driveway and street from inside the kitchen and breakfast room. It also had small windows that were just like holes punched in a stone wall, making it feel somewhat like a fortress. Wanting to open up their home and make it seem more welcoming, the owners hired an architect to define the entry and increase its appeal. Inspired by the style of Mediterranean casas, the architect began the process by designing a courtyard—a gracious, lingering space defined by a shapely wall and captivating decorative archway. On the driveway side, he added a small planter shelf to soften the wall, as well as a glazed tile panel for a quiet infusion of color. On the courtyard side, he sent the wall pouring into a soothing fountain, creating a blissful environment for all who enter.

The floor of the courtyard was covered in Mexican terra cotta while the brick corners of the house were replaced by stucco quoins. As with the back wall of the entry and the wall in the breakfast room, the conversion from brick to stucco was intended to reinforce the Mediterranean influence. Colorful plantings and new larger windows completed the courtyard space, giving it a spirited facelift that enlivens the entire home.

LEFT, AFTER The new arched entry, flanked by lush landscaping and a trickling fountain, beckons guests with newfound grandeur.

OPPOSITE BOTTOM, BEFORE An overwhelming mishmash of textures converged in the entryway of this home, leaving it feeling cold, hard, and unwelcoming.

OPPOSITE TOP, AFTER Pre-cast picture frames add dimension to the entry wall, surrounding textured stucco and a custom-designed wooden mailbox.

Using Water to Create a More Pleasing Landscape

Even the best of neighbors can sometimes come too close for comfort, invading your privacy and your property in a way that makes life miserable. Such was the case for the owners of this backyard, a small, verdant space that resonated with the annoying sound of the neighbor's air conditioning compressor. Always noisy and never private, the yard was in dire need of a quick fix—and that's what the architect provided. Limited in square footage and hard-pressed to muffle the sound of the air conditioner, he looked to the soothing sounds of water to solve the problem, creating a waterfall that would deflect the constant hum.

Designed to be exactly as wide as the nearby swimming pool, the waterfall not only fills the space with serene cascading water, but also visually expands the yard and makes it feel larger. A pump behind the poured concrete forms collects water from the pool and recirculates it, sending it tumbling back to the pool for a dynamic tumbling sound that's music to the ears.

LEFT, BEFORE Though well enclosed and bursting with garden delights, this otherwise pleasant backyard was sullied by the irritating sounds of the neighbor's air conditioner.

OPPOSITE TOP, AFTER The neutral tone of the concrete allows the waterfall to slip easily into the background, ensuring that it will never distract from the overall landscape.

OPPOSITE BOTTOM, AFTER Proving that paradise can abound in even the smallest spaces, this petite backyard offers a wide array of tactile pleasures.

The soothing sounds of water can make any garden feel more tranquil.

Expressing Individuality with an Outdoor Sculpture Garden

Having a home that intimately reflects your interests and provides a sense of security is no small order, but that's what the owners of this international-style townhouse were looking for. As first-time parents who also happened to be art collectors living in a very artsy neighborhood, they commissioned an architect to transform their home into a unique work of sculpture. Wanting to buffer street noise and boost privacy, they asked him to create an inner courtyard that could serve as a tranquil garden as well as a secure entrance to their front door.

He responded by designing a sculptural wall with a stainless steel gate, following a 2-1-3 rhythm composed of overlapping and piercing shapes. To make the wall less forbidding, he created a small circle in it, filling the cavity with steel tubes that mimicked the angular pattern in the gate. A concrete bench was inlaid with ceramic tiles to infuse the space with color along with energetic dashes of red-orange in the pavers. Meditative and highly personal, the courtyard is now a charming complement to its owners' vibrant lifestyle.

LEFT, AFTER Intersecting shapes form the outline of the new courtyard, suiting the existing architecture to a tee.

RIGHT, BEFORE The direct access to the heart of this home made the owners feel vulnerable while the lifeless entry proved unappealing for guests.

BELOW, AFTER Artwork and plant life mingle easily in this contemplative space, offering a calming respite from the outside world.

Choosing Details That Can Stand the Test of Time

Advice from the Architect...

If you want to guess the age of a home, look at the style of the roof and the windows. A shed roof says 1960s, a mansard roof says 1970s. Narrow fascias at the end of a roof overhang were prominent in the '50s and '60s, but later on, bigger fascias became desirable. Large picture windows, which were popular from the 1940s until the 1970s, suddenly disappeared with the energy crisis. Now, with the advent of double-paned and "low E" glass, larger windows are being used again.

TOP LEFT, BEFORE The owners of this backyard pool and spa felt that something about the patio design wasn't quite right, but they couldn't figure out what it was.

BOTTOM LEFT, BEFORE An eagle-eyed architect spotted the snag almost immediately, zeroing in on the shape and style of the columns holding up the porch.

ABOVE The hip, modern style of this beachfront home demanded fun and freshness even down to the smallest details, including this sculptural outdoor shower with a lively sense of humor.

Reimagining a Drab Front Entry

All the personality had drained out of this 1960s split level many years ago, leaving the owners eager for an update. A young professional couple with three small boys, they wanted their home to reflect the casual nature of their lifestyle as well as blend in with the general vibe of the neighborhood. As is, it had no foyer and no sense of entry, so they asked an architect to reinvision the front façade, making it grander, friendlier, and more clearly defined.

He decided to build the elevation around a theme, imagining a warm, genial gathering space similar to a courtyard. Dividing the home into four levels inside, he dressed the outside with peaked gables, matching dormer windows and aluminum gridded windows. He also carried out the gabled theme in the front door and custom mailbox, both of which feature a wide center breastplate and grid pattern made from birds-eye maple. Intent on using cohesive design elements throughout the house, he formed the transom above the door into the same shape as the gable ends and dormers, and with these changes, the front entry blossomed into a gracious ingress, allowing the family to welcome guests with ease.

LEFT, BEFORE Despite resting desirably close to a beautiful waterway, this tired mid-century home lacked the charm and character that its young owners desired.

ABOVE, AFTER Thoughtful landscaping and a newly laid brick driveway add to the unique appeal of this redesigned façade.

OPPOSITE, AFTER The soft, buttery tone of the maple front door spices up this otherwise neutral palette, infusing it with richness and depth.

PART TWO:
Secrets of a Successful Renovation

Traffic Flow

If your home has a poorly designed layout, you'll know it pretty quickly. Disruptive traffic flow appears in many forms, all of which make the experience of living in your home less than ideal. Do you recognize any of these problems?

- While trying to watch a TV show from your favorite chair, family members constantly walk in front of you on their way to other rooms.
- An open door swings right into a busy pathway, causing you to wait until it's closed before you can pass.
- In scrambling for seats in the breakfast room, your kids shift the chairs around, leaving them to block the walkway.
- Your kitchen is so cramped and busy that it's nearly impossible to prepare a meal without a dozen interruptions.

Sometimes proper traffic flow can be achieved by simply rearranging furniture or solving storage issues, but often it requires a total reworking of the existing floor plan. Homes today simply don't function in the same way that they did fifty or even fifteen years ago, so a layout that worked then may not be efficient now. Modern families demand dedicated space for media equipment and computers but they tend to have less need for formal living and dining rooms. Current trends also call for larger, more open spaces than in the past, allowing rooms to flow gently into one another rather than stop and start abruptly. With proper traffic flow, all these ideals can be met without compromising the ease at which you move throughout your house or share the space with others.

FAR LEFT, BEFORE Never mind the big, weird light fixture. This kitchen's biggest problem was the fact that its refrigerator door swung open into the doorway—an obvious traffic flow faux pas.

LEFT, BEFORE Bifold doors, while not as obtrusive as full-swing doors, can still impede a walkway, such as the case with this poorly positioned pantry.

ABOVE, AFTER A well defined eating area and careful use of space substantially increased the efficiency of this kitchen. The triangular layout of the appliances allows for ease of movement while the wide open central walkway easily accommodates the chef of the day and several others.

OPPOSITE, AFTER An abundance of storage—in the form of drawers, cabinets, and multiple display shelves—means that clutter will not have an impact on traffic flow. By keeping everything in its place, it is assured that this kitchen will function well even when crowded with guests.

Proper Lighting

Fill a home with sunshine and it immediately feels lighter, brighter, and more cheerful. That's why it's essential that every room receive a healthy dose of natural light during the day. Renovation offers several ways to achieve this, including adding or enlarging windows, adding a glass-paneled exterior door, or installing a skylight—though none of these can help with illumination at night. After the sun goes down, look to the following three types of electric lighting for creating the most pleasant and functional atmosphere.

GENERAL LIGHTING

This is the barebones ceiling fixture that every room should have, though many modern homes are often built without it. If you don't have at least one general light per room, you need one.

TASK LIGHTING

Ideal for kitchen countertops or any other work surface, task lighting allows you to do just that—complete tasks. It should be bright enough for you to see well in a small, spotlighted area, though when displayed en masse it can also illuminate a large area. Options include halogen, low-voltage xenon, and low-cost fluorescent. Canned or pendant lights installed above a sink or stove can also serve as task lighting.

AMBIENT LIGHTING

More decorative than functional, ambient lighting nonetheless serves an important purpose in that it sets the mood in a room, making it feel more intimate and cozy. Table lamps, paper lanterns, candles, and "just for show" fixtures are all varieties of ambient lighting. A "general" ceiling fixture can also fit the bill when equipped with a dimmer switch.

When choosing lighting for a room, consider that pale colors and shiny surfaces reflect ambient light, meaning that a space with fairer tones will require less light than one with dark or matte-finish surfaces. It's also important to use brighter lights in tall rooms to avoid shadows, but opt for softer lights in low-ceilinged spaces, where reflections tend to bounce off walls.

LEFT, BEFORE When sunlight and space are in short supply, homeowners often turn to mirrors for added effect, though rarely with as much gusto as the misguided decorator behind this dated bathroom.

OPPOSITE, AFTER A proper balance of natural and artificial light serves this bathroom much more effectively, giving it a warm, welcoming glow while also providing ample illumination for daily grooming.

Good Design

A renovation is an investment in the future value of your home, so it's wise to make design choices that will still feel fresh and functional ten years down the road. Here's how:

STICK WITH NEUTRALS

Many color-loving homeowners are compelled to infuse every room with a bold burst of red or fuchsia, but what they don't realize is that they're committing themselves to those colors and that look for many years. A smarter game plan involves using neutrals on expensive-to-change items such as floors, countertops, and tilework, and then choosing vivid hues when it comes to furniture and accessories.

CREATE A SENSE OF CONTINUITY

Often a homeowner will remodel one room individually, with no thought as to how it flows with adjoining spaces. It's ideal to rework multiple rooms all at once but if that's not possible there are still ways to create unity. The easiest is to use similar materials or colors throughout the house, weaving a common thread from one space to the next. If you have maple cabinets in the kitchen, for example, use maple trim in the dining room. The idea is not to make each space identical, but rather to add colors, textures, and materials that repeat in subtle ways.

THINK FUNCTION FIRST

Before you fall in love with a room layout on paper, consider the most basic question—where will all the furniture go? If you have too many large windows, you may struggle to find a spot for your sofa or TV. Or if your new space will be wide open with few walls, you might find it difficult to position your bed. Try to imagine exactly how you'll live in the new room—furniture, pets, kids, books, and electronics included—before agreeing to any major changes.

ABOVE TOP, BEFORE Everybody has a corner in their home that's not being well utilized, like this catch-all space where a variety of hobbies and interests seem to converge.

ABOVE BOTTOM, BEFORE This too-big bookcase illustrates another element of good design: scale and proportion. To harmonize with its environment, a sofa, window, doorway, molding, or any other component of a room must fit in terms of size and visual weight.

OPPOSITE, AFTER A problem area becomes a well-appointed asset with this handsome corner bar, where wood tones and materials used throughout the house are repeated for the sake of continuity.

PART THREE:

Close to Home—The Architect's Most Personal Projects

A Family Room

BELOW, BEFORE A large but disjointed space with no real plan, Barry's cousin's family room would need a complete overhaul to take advantage of its obvious assets.

RIGHT, AFTER By replacing a traditional archway with a more contemporary support, Barry dramatically opened up the family room and gave it a strong central feature. Allowing the beauty of the ocean to serve as a focal point, he built the palette around honey-toned maple and neutral taupe furniture, enlivening the space in a subtle way with vibrant artwork, striking angles, and warm ambient lighting. The unique media cabinet on one wall not only provides storage but also stands as a sculptural piece all on its own.

A room's strongest asset, such as a beautiful view, should always guide the design.

The Architect's Bedroom

RIGHT, BEFORE Barry's master bedroom had no distinctive personality save its one corner window, which did little to boost the sense of style.

BELOW, AFTER Artwork takes center stage in the new master bedroom, where drywall build-outs along the walls bring added depth and character. Even the headboard is crafted from drywall, allowing Barry and Barbara to maintain their love of clean-lined, no-fuss furniture. Once again, the palette is neutral but the accessories are pulsing with color.

The Master Bathroom

LEFT, BEFORE A choppy, compartmentalized space with an L-shaped layout, the old master bathroom offered a wealth of square footage but most of it was awkwardly arranged and not very user-friendly.

ABOVE, AFTER "I establish a theme and keep repeating it," Barry says, explaining the thread of splashy blue woven into the new master suite. Inspired by a bold sea-toned abstract painting, he chose aqueous tiles for the back wall of the glass-enclosed shower and then continued the palette in smaller ways on the floor and in the sink area. A fresh new layout, much more open than before, makes the bold palette seem comfortable rather than overpowering

An Inside Job

The transformation of Barry Sugerman's Miami home began like any other renovation, with one small difference. As an architect, Barry knew exactly what he was getting into. The 1956 ranch house that he shares with his wife, Barbara, had been poorly remodeled three times prior, leaving ceilings low, spaces chopped up, and the beautiful view of Biscayne Bay completely ignored. "Our challenge was to bring the house into the twenty-first century, but we also needed to maintain its structural integrity and original charm," he explains. "Each previous remodel had been less inspired than its predecessor, so we had an awful lot of work to do."

The Architect's Living Room

RIGHT, BEFORE Isolated in a dark, interior section of the house, the living room suffered from poor lighting, a low ceiling, and heavy vintage details that didn't agree with Barry and Barbara's contemporary aesthetic.

ABOVE, AFTER By removing every other joist, doubling up remaining joists, and adding new cross members, Barry created an alluring coffered ceiling that gives the illusion of greater height. Almost unrecognizable from its previous incarnation, the new living room positively buzzes with life and personality. A lone panel of bold red paint adds punch to the otherwise neutral space, drawing greater attention to the colors and shapes within the Sugermans' diverse art collection.

The Sugerman's Pool

LEFT, BEFORE This tranquil pool area might have been fine for most people, but to an architect it lacked visual interest. It also offered little in the way of eye candy for passersby in Biscayne Bay.

BELOW, AFTER Deepening the fascia on the rear elevation was not going to be sufficient enough to give it real character, so Barry took his design one step further. For the sheer delight of visitors and neighboring homeowners, he built a dramatic arch that sends water gently tumbling into the pool below.

The Front Façade

BELOW, AFTER: Without altering the roofline, Barry was able to raise the ceilings inside by removing the bottom chord of the stick-built roof trusses. What did change outside were the soffits—which dropped down and became more streamlined—and the overall color of the house, which took on a soothing blue tone.

INSET, BEFORE: A well-manicured and welcoming entry, the original façade's only problem was that it didn't match the modern tastes of its owners.

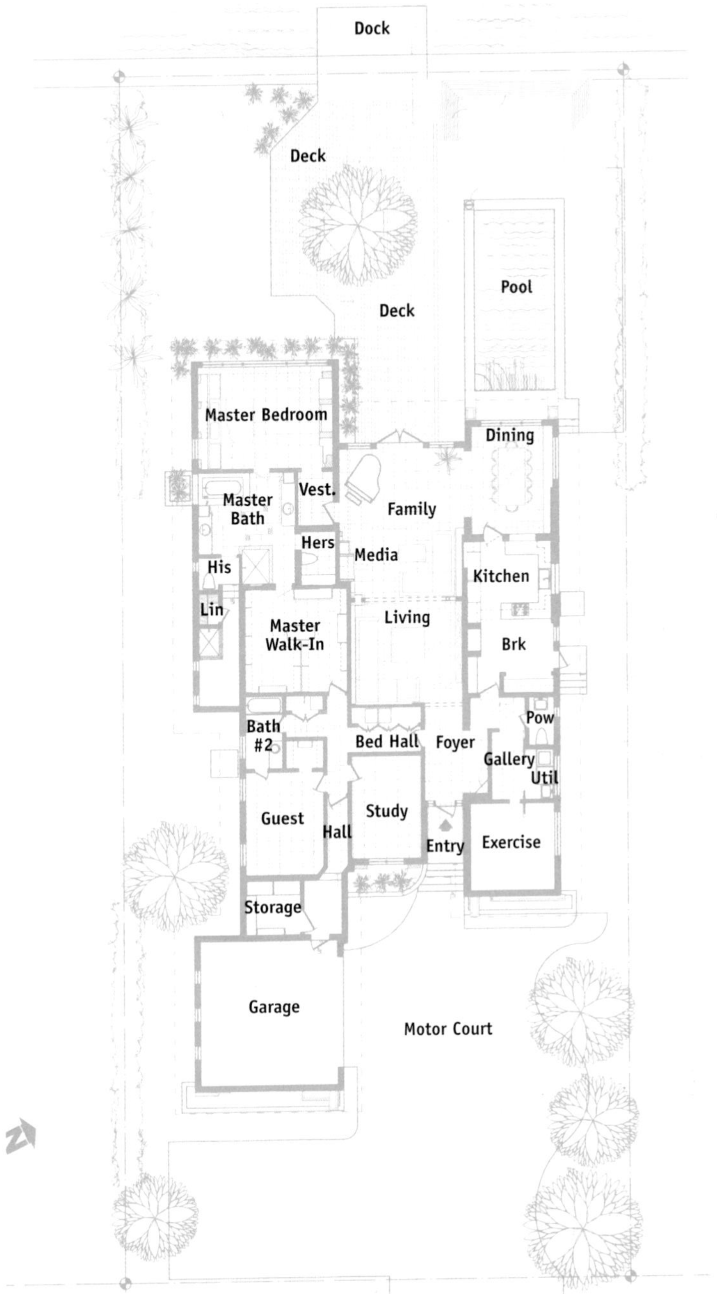
Dock
Deck
Deck
Pool
Master Bedroom
Dining
Master Bath
Vest.
Family
Hers
Media
His
Kitchen
Lin
Master Walk-In
Living
Brk
Bath #2
Bed Hall
Foyer
Pow
Gallery
Util
Guest
Hall
Study
Entry
Exercise
Storage
Garage
Motor Court

The Floor Plan

LEFT, BEFORE Originally the house had three zones going from right to left—service, living, and sleeping. That's a good sign for anyone wanting to remodel because it means that the basic tenets of good space planning were heeded right from the beginning. A wall or two might have to be moved, but all in all, the layout is very functional.

RIGHT, AFTER Over a period of eight months, Barry and Barbara refashioned nearly every inch of their home, making it more vibrant, more efficient, and ultimately more in tune with their needs and lifestyle. "In transforming this house, not one square foot was added," he says proudly. "Only heart and soul."

GLOSSARY

Baluster
One of the upright, usually rounded or vase-shaped supports, of a balustrade. A post in a balustrade of a bridge or a flight of stairs.

Balustrade
A rail and the row of balusters or posts that support it, as on a balcony.

Barrel-Vault
A vault having the form of a very deep arch. Also called barrel-roof, cradle-vault, tunnel-vault, wagon-roof, or wagon-vault.

Bearing Wall
Any of the walls supporting the roof or a floor or of a building.

Bullnose
A rounded edge, corner, or projection, as on a stairstep or paving stone.

Cantilever
A projecting structure, such as a beam, that is supported at one end and carries a load at the other end or along its length. A member, such as a beam, that projects beyond a fulcrum and is supported by a balancing member or a downward force behind the fulcrum. A bracket or block supporting a balcony or cornice.

Chord
A line segment that joins two points on a curve. Also the structural members of a wood truss.

Coffered
To form (as a ceiling) with recessed panels.

Crown Molding
The sculptured wood trim that is normally applied to the wall at or near the point where the walls meet the ceiling.

Façade
The front of a building; also, any face of a building given special architectural treatment.

Fascia
A flat horizontal band or member between moldings.

Gable
The generally triangular section of wall at the end of a pitched roof, occupying the space between the two slopes of the roof. A triangular, usually ornamental architectural section, as one above an arched door or window.

Girder
A beam of steel, wood, or reinforced concrete used as a main horizontal support in a building or bridge.

Halogens
A gas-filled, high-intensity lamp that produces full-spectrum light, which appears brighter than limited spectrum incandescent output and causes less eye-strain.

Knee Brace
A diagonal support placed across the angle between two members that are joined; serves to stiffen and strengthen the members.

Low E (low-emittance) Coating
Microscopically thin, virtually invisible, metal or metallic oxide layers deposited on a window or skylight primarily to reduce heat.

Mansard Roof
A roof having two slopes on all sides with the lower slope steeper than the upper.

Quoin (also Coign)
An exterior angle of a wall or other piece of masonry. Any of the stones used in forming such an angle, often being of large size and dressed or arranged so as to form a decorative contrast with the adjoining walls.

Sapele Pommele
An exotic African wood ranging in color from medium red to purple-brown. Also known as sapelewood, aboudikrou, sapelli, sipo, sapele mahogany, tiama, Gold Coast cedar, penkwa, and libuyu.

Shed roof
A roof having a single slope.

Soffit
The underside of a structural component, such as a beam, arch, staircase, or cornice.

Stucco
A durable finish for exterior walls, usually composed of cement, sand, and lime, and applied while wet. A fine plaster for interior wall ornamentation, such as moldings.

Sustainable
The movement associated with environmentally conscious architectural design.

Task Lighting
Lighting that serves a limited area where a person's work is concentrated.

Truss
A rigid framework, as of wooden beams or metal bars, designed to support a structure, such as a roof.

ARCHITECTURAL REFERENCES

American Institute of Architects
800-AIA-3837
www.aia.org

American Society of Home Inspectors
800-743-ASHI
www.ashi.org

Barry Sugerman, Architect
12801 NE 7th Avenue
North Miami, FL 33161 USA
305-893-6055
www.barrysugerman.com

Better Business Bureau
www.bbb.org

International Code Council
For information on building codes
888-ICC-SAFE
www.iccsafe.org

PHOTOGRAPHER CREDITS

All photographs by Robert Stein with the exception of the following:

Dan Forer, 7 (top); 8; 14; 15; 48; 49; 61 (top); 66; 67 (bottom); 81; 119; 120; 139; 146 (bottom); 151 (top); 153 (bottom); 154

Barry Sugerman, 10; 12; 17 (top & bottom, left); 18; 20; 24; 26; 28; 31; 34; 37; 45 (top); 50; 54; 60 (bottom); 61 (bottom); 62 (top); 63 (bottom); 65 (top); 67 (top, left & right); 70; 72; 74; 76 (top); 78; 80; 82; 84; 87 (top); 88 (top); 89 (bottom); 94 (top); 96; 98; 100; 102; 105 (inset); 106; 108 (top); 109 (bottom); 110 (top); 113 (left); 114; 117 (inset); 118; 121 (top); 123 (top); 126; 129 (bottom); 130; 133 (top); 134 (top); 136 (bottom); 140 (bottom, left & right); 142; 144; 148; 150 (top); 151 (bottom); 153 (top); 154 (inset)

Mark Surloff, 6 (bottom); 16; 51; 52; 101; 122; 124; 125; 128; 129 (top); 131; 132; 133 (bottom); 135; 145; 150 (bottom); 152 (top)

ACKNOWLEDGMENTS

This book was made possible by my wife, Barbara, whose patience, insight, and contributions to my life are immeasurable. To Alexa Rossy, for taking my words and turning them into a cohesive manuscript that I could submit to a publisher. To Diego Lastres, whose artistic abilities and computer genius took my vast and varied collection of projects and organized them in an interesting and understandable way. To Natalia Carr, whose patience, advice, and organizational skills helped pull the whole book together. To my friends Art Pyle, Candido Quintana, Leslie Wynne, Yvonne Eldon, and Brenda Lanza, who helped conceive and produce the work displayed in this book. And to my good friends Marshall Ames and Mark Grodin, who not only encouraged me to keep this project going but who also had the confidence to commission me to do some of my best work on their own houses.

–Barry Sugerman

To my publisher, Winnie Prentiss, photo editor, Betsy Gammons, and beloved husband, Keith Howard: thank you all for your patience and support during this project. Without your encouragement and laughter, I could not have risen to the challenge. Thanks also to Natalia Carr, whose amazing organizational skills made my job so much easier.

–Shannon Howard

ABOUT THE AUTHORS

Barry Sugerman, architect, A.I.A. grew up in Miami Beach, Florida. A graduate of Georgia Tech, he has been practicing architecture since 1965 with projects in such diverse locations as Florida and the Florida Keys; Big Sky, Montana; Dallas and Houston, Texas; Savannah, Georgia; Tegucigalpa, Honduras; and Adana, Turkey.

Specializing in designing custom homes, both new and remodeled, and providing services including architecture and interior design, Sugerman has been widely featured in local and national magazines. He has won more than 140 regional and national awards for both new and remodeled residences, including the Golden Aurora Award for a Mediterranean-style residence, judged best home in the southeastern United States.

Sugerman lives with his wife, Barbara, and dog, Sugar, in Bay Harbor, Florida, with regular visits from his three children and grandchildren. He does not consider architecture to be his profession, but rather his way of life.

Shannon Howard is a lifestyle writer and scout for an eclectic array of interior design magazines, including *Country Living*, *Midwest Living*, and *Decor*. She's also the author of *Southern Rooms II: The Timeless Beauty of the American South*, published by Quarry Books in 2005. Her writing and marketing company, Colossal Creative (www.colossalcreative.net), is based in St. Louis, Missouri.